Mind Fucking Mindfully

A Guide to Mental Manipulation for BDSM and Sadomasochism

Figure 1. Tortured with Compliments

Mindfucking Mindfully

A Guide to Mental Manipulation for BDSM and Sadomasochism

By Sir Ezra

First Edition

Mindfucking Mindfully: A Guide To Mental Manipulation For BDSM and Sadomasochism
Copyright © 2021 by Sir Ezra Algos

All rights reserved. No part of this book may be reproduced or transmitted in any form or by any means without written permission from the author.

ISBN (978-1-7372180-9-8)

Dedication

To my beautiful slave wife Queen Ana. Your love and support have made it possible for me to reach for the fulfillment of my wildest dreams. Your love represents the most compassion, patience, understanding, and intimacy that I have known in my life. Without you, this book is the least of things that would not have been possible.

"All warfare is based on deception. Therefore, when capable feign incapacity, when active, inactivity. When near, make it appear that you are far away; when far away, that you are near. Offer the enemy bait to lure him; feign disorder and strike him. When he concentrates, prepare against him; where he is strong, avoid him. Pretend inferiority and encourage his arrogance."
 -Sun Tzu from The Art of War written in 5th century BCE China.

Table of Contents

Section 0 Front stuff	**1**
Dedication	5
Epigraph	6
Table of Contents	7
Forward	10
Preface	11
Acknowledgments	13
Section 1 Introduction	**14**
Why I Am Writing This Book	14
Why More People Don't Teach it	15
A Note About Interludes	17
Interlude #1 Fake Gutting	18
Section 2 *Mindfucking* in BDSM	**21**
Mindfucking as a Sexual Practice	21
Types of *Mindfucking*	23
Interlude #2 Devil's Tube Gag	29
Disclaimer - One Size Not Fitting All	30
The History of Mindfucking	31
Differentiating BDSM from Abuse	37
Interlude #3 Lex's Phone a friend	39
Common Practice	40
Mindfucking for D/s	41
Interlude #4 Power of the Written Word	44
Mindfucking in Role-Play	48
Interlude #5 Truth Serum	49
Mindfucking for Sadists	51
Interlude #6 Midori's Argument with the Dungeon Monitor	53
Section 3 Unethical, non-consensual, or unerotic Mindfucking	**55**

Mindfucking Vs. *Mindfucking*	55
Mindfucking in Accademia	56
Mindfucking in Politics	59
Mindfucking for the Political Underdog	61
Mindfucking in Corporate Culture	62
Mindfucking in Sales and Marketing	64

Section 4 Safety and Ethics — 69

Cautions and Warnings	69
Interlude #7 Monsignor Hollywood & the Shit Sack	71
Trauma Informed Mindfucking	72
Negotiating Trauma Informed Play	74
Interlude #8 Sox Gets What's Coming	74
Ethical Considerations	76
Interlude #9 Monsignor Hollywood and the Clairvoyant Insight	79
Interlude #10 Midori's Chainsaw Scene	81
Therapeutic Potential	82
Interlude #11 Spider in a Jar	85

Section 5 Doing the thing — 88

Negotiating a *Mindfuck*	88
Conditional Ask with Explanation	89
Making Negotiation Sexy	91
Interlude #12 Monsignor Hollywood And the Rubber Masks	95
Aftercare	97
Interlude #13 Mistress Cyan and the Skills Test	101
Kinky Blackjack	102
Sir Ezra's Box	110
Interlude #14 Philip K Dick Move	118
Conclusion	123
References Resources & Bibliography	127

-content in this book is meant for entertainment purposes only-

Forward

This is a terrible book.
Why is this terrible? Because it shares all the sweet secrets that we, mindfuckers, have up our sleeves. (Dammit, Ezra!)
This is a childish book. Why is this Childish? Because this gives us the tools to play like the wicked little children we once were, and still are.
(Redrum! Redrum! Come play with me. - says my adorable little inner child to you.)
This is an adult book. (no, you filthy minded reader, not THAT kind of adult. I mean adult, as in grown up)
Why is it adult? Because this takes into consideration the wide range of people doing our BDSM thing for so many different lusts and fantasies.
(Ok, so the fantasies are THAT kind of adult content.)
This is a humane book.
Why is it humane? Because this tries very hard to address the gray area of desire. This gives several very useful tools to think about, discuss, and use for understanding consent, fun, agency, and abuse.
(Go Humans! Unless that is you're playing as an alien captor.)
Have a terribly childish nerdy grown-ass humane devil of a good time!
-Midori

Preface

It is tempting to litter this book with things that mess with the reader by saying phrases like "You are now manually breathing." I simply won't do that. Saying things like "You are now hearing this in Morgan Freeman's voice" might be described a mindfuck in the most popular definition, but it strays outside of what we will define as a mindfuck. We define mindfucking as an ethical, consensual, and erotic practice which must be negotiated. Though the content of this book, centers on methods of manipulation, is not meant to manipulate the reader.

That being said, aspects of this book may be seen as distasteful or even disturbing to some. The following text simply isn't for everyone. If you don't like it feel free to put it down. If you put it down, feel free to pick it back up. Lastly, if anything in this book describes activities in your life but lacks the essential negotiation, consent, and aftercare, please seek a professional's help and do your best to remove yourself from the abusive situation. Conversely, if you find that some behaviors that you have done are described in this book and again lack the essential negotiation, consent, and aftercare, then I urge you to inspect your behavior with the assistance of a counselor, therapist, or psychiatrist in order to safeguard your friends and family from what are likely abusive behaviors.

Acknowledgments

Thanks to those who shared their stories or artwork:

Midori, Danarama, Monsignor Hollywood, Queen Ana, Devil, Durant, Tracy, Sunny Megatron, Rosie, Suburbanmystic, Candy, David, FetishArtist.net, Slicer, Scotty Dog, Foxes in Love, Mistress Cyan, Lex, and all the lovely people who let my fuck with their mind through the years.

Section 1

Introduction

Why I am writing this book

Erotic Mindfucking is a form of edgeplay that is part of the global subculture of BDSM. By its broadest definition it is so widely practiced that many people are doing it without so much as knowing it. Furthermore, it is one of the most difficult practices in BDSM to distinguish from abuse. Many people feel apprehension when teaching this subject because it could enable bad actors.

I felt it was important to put what I have learned in one place in writing because, as the global BDSM community blossoms and the veil of shame lifts everywhere, more people will be trying out erotic mindfucking. As powerful as it is, they should have the resources to practice as safely as possible.

Lastly, I imagine that this book will be an unexpected resource for people who have unknowingly been on the receiving end of emotional or psychological abuse. In this text we describe behaviors that when not preceded by negotiation and followed by aftercare are unhealthy and unsafe. If you recognize that you were in, or are currently in a situation where you are receiving any kind of abuse, I hope that you can find your way to safety. It may be helpful to utilize professional third parties such as therapists, counselors, psychiatrists or case managers to reduce the risk of any further harm to yourself or loved ones around you. Those interested in kink-friendly therapists or other resources can see page 126 for more information.

***

Why More People Don't Teach *Mindfucking*

I recall in the early days of my BDSM exploration, I was drawn to *mindfucking*, but it was challenging to find educational resources. I remember that people would refuse to teach me about the subject because I was new to the scene. One person even told me, "If you are *really* interested, go look up emotional abuse tactics." That was *terrible* advice, because it did not grant me access to the contextual knowledge surrounding the practices in the BDSM community.

To illustrate the preposterousness of this approach, allow me to draw an analogy. Imagine if I were interested in learning about erotic knife play. Because I am new, no one will tell me much about it. Eventually, after asking around, someone says to me "If you *really* want to learn about erotic knife play, go look up surgical techniques." Again, this is a terrible piece of advice, because it denies the learner the contextual knowledge that comes when learning within the BDSM community.

To continue the analogy one step further, if I looked up surgical techniques, yes, I would learn about how to do cutting and perhaps sutures as well, but I have missed a lot of contextual and cultural information. *Most* knife play is more about sensation and dramatics than cutting. I personally enjoy frequent erotic knife play in my relationships and I rarely intentionally break skin, save for a special occasion once or twice a year.

What I hope to communicate to you here is that like knife play, there are many ways to practice erotic mindfucking that minimize the risks while maximizing the fun. There are lots of ways to do saf*er* mindfucking that can help you and your partner(s) have sexy good fun without driving the knife too deep so to speak.

Similar to knife play, erotic mindfucking is considered edge play, because it can easily cause harm. Due to the high level of risk involved, many people are not comfortable teaching it to others. I believe this is appropriate. I don't think anyone should teach if they are apprehensive, and it is at the teacher's discretion to decide what they are or are not willing to teach.

***

A Note About Interludes

When I set out to write this book, I was very aware of the possibility to be lost in the intellectual. This book is not about the theoretical or the hypothetical. It is about the actual, the practical. I hope we can remember throughout the text that *mindfucking* is something that is practiced between sexual partners all across the globe. For this reason, I will be including a number of stories that were either my own personal experience or the personal experience of those I have spoken to. These are a contrast to the erotica you might have read on the subject which rarely takes into account safety and ethics.

It is important to remember that we are talking about things that actually happen. *Mindfucking* is not some abstract notion. In our case, it is an actual practice. All of the interludes describe experiences people have had first hand. Some may be easily replicated at home, while others, being more elaborate or dangerous, should be left to the more experienced players. Do only what you feel comfortable doing and what feels like fun to do. Some names have been changed for the sake of privacy. Other names are people's scene names that they use to maintain some level of anonymity.

***

Interlude #1 Fake Gutting

This *mindfuck* is one that I really like because it always elicits a strong reaction that makes me cackle maniacally. I've done it many times in scenes that involved knife play but my favorite time was when I was teaching a *mindfuck* class at Los Angeles' Threshold Society.

In the packed main room, I had my friend Slicer with me at center stage. I pulled him aside before the beginning of the class and asked if I could use him for a demonstration. I used the spamming technique to get specific consent while still maintaining the surprise of the *mindfuck*. More on spamming can be found in the Section 5 Doing the Thing on page 88.

I showed him my folding knife, which I had been playing with for most of the beginning of the class. I asked him to hold it and make sure it was real and sharp as we faced the audience. Then I asked him to give it back to me, and I closed it as I placed it in my back pocket. I began to change the subject, seeming to ignore the knife. Then I reached into my back pocket again and pulled out a different knife that looked similar.

Without so much as looking down at the new knife in my hand I lunged at Slicer. With one hand on his shoulder to pull him close and with the other, I jammed the knife right into his gut again and again. The new knife I pulled out was actually a trick knife where the dull plastic blade retracts into the handle with any pressure at all.

He doubled over and let out the most wonderful sound. It was halfway between a grunt and a scream. I now know exactly what he would sound like if he were to be knifed to death, at least at first. The sound still echoes in my mind bringing a smile to my sadistic face even now, more than a year later.

Of course, he was unharmed by this. The blade safely retracted into the handle and left him with not so much as a scratch. He got a jolt of adrenaline and I got a good laugh about it. The class got to see what a more extreme *mindfuck* could look like even if it only lasted a few seconds.

I would describe this as an illusion *mindfuck,* possibly also humiliating. It was certainly an illusion because he was under the impression it was a real knife in my hand. After all, he had lots of reason to believe that was the case considering he had just been inspecting a real knife a moment earlier. It is possibly degrading or humiliating but that depends on the subject. If he found it humiliating to have been "stabbed" on stage or to have made that noise then it was a humiliating *mindfuck* for him.

Section 2

Mindfucking in BDSM

Mindfucking As A Sexual Practice

The word mindfuck can be used to describe many activities, but in this book, we will focus on the use of the word specific to BDSM and ethical, consensual, erotic activity. *Mindfucking* is a practice common among sadomasochists that is part of sexual play. When I refer to sexual play, it is in the BDSM sense. This may involve the lead up to penetrative sex, or could involve sexualized activity that excludes penetrative sex entirely. In this text we go into detail describing both the real-life account of people as they have experienced *mindfucks,* and an intellectual dissection of the practice so we can better understand how to do it and how not to do it.

Mindfuck with the italicization will be used when I am referring to activity that is consensual, ethical, and erotic. When I use mindfuck without italics I will be referring to any activity which is either unethical, non-consensual, and or un-erotic. The mindfuck will be explored separately as it is essential to healthy BDSM that we are capable of distinguishing BDSM from abuse.

What *mindfucking* is not, specifically in the context of this book, is non-consensual manipulation by an individual, group or organization, manipulation with malice (even if it is consensual), a puzzle or conundrum, something aimed at disturbing, confusing, or altering the perception of reality of *unwilling or unwitting* participants. It is also not that kind of enlightening or positive experience that can be described as a "positive mindfuck."

What we will be using the word *mindfuck* to describe is any techniques used to consensually excite, arouse, or manipulate one's partner (or partners) for mutual benefit. The result may be sexy, scary, disturbing, upsetting, gross, build antici...

...pation, create feelings of empowerment, disempowerment, degrade, ennoble, or lead to any other state of mind deemed desirable by the parties involved.

As with any other activity in BDSM, the key differences that distinguish these activities from abuse are the use of negotiation and aftercare. It is important that these activities have a discreet end time. Since aftercare must be done after the activity, there must be a discrete ending. If not, it can be unclear when aftercare needs to begin. For those interested in learning more on differentiating BDSM from abuse later in Section 2 on page 37.

In Section 3, "Unethical, Non-consensual, and Unerotic Mindfucking" (page 550, I will explore just as the title suggests, mindfucking in the world as it contrasts to our definition in BDSM. This is useful because it helps us understand when we are being abused by individuals or organizations. It also helps us understand the themes that we may be drawn to and where we first experienced them.

***

Types of *Mindfucking*

The following is a categorization of *mindfucking* that I propose to better understand what is happening in the examples given. No such categorization is in popular use and I recognize that there is room for improvement moving forward.

Figure 2. An Example of an Expectation *Mindfuck* by Fetishartist.net

Very few *mindfucks* will be easily described by just one category. As you will see in our various interludes, most *mindfucks* can be described by at least two categories. The purpose for using this categorization is to better illustrate what is the mechanism of a given *mindfuck*.

The Types of *Mindfuck* Include:
- Expectation
- Perceived power
- Illusions
- Asymmetric information
- Perspective alteration
- Degrading or Ennobling
- Humiliation

If you need a pneumonic to remember all of the types of *minfucks* described here I would suggest "piphead".

Expectation *mindfucks* are ones that play with your partner's expectations. This is any kind of play where you set false or unclear expectations to manipulate your partner. This could be as simple as establishing a pattern and then deviating from that pattern without warning. Or you could get consent for something you have no plan on doing. Another quick example might be setting out a toy during play time to imply you are going to use it when you have no intention of doing so.

Perceived power *mindfucks* are ones where your partner is made to think you have power you do not or confuse the power you do have. You could, for example, explain to your partner that you have magic powers. This type of *mindfuck* could also be used in a way to hide power that you do have by giving the impression it is up to someone else or up to chance.

Illusion *mindfucks* are ones that use a stimulus that is likely to be wrongly perceived or interpreted by the senses. You could for example play the Shepard's Tone, an auditory illusion that gives the impression that a sound is indefinitely raising in pitch, to create anxiety in your partner, or switch a real knife out for a fake one.

Asymmetric information *mindfucks* are those that use a disparity in knowledge to affect a partner. An example of this could be telling your partner that you know what they did and letting them stew without further explanation. Another example is having your partner fill out a fetish survey and give you the answers. You may get the answers from them but not provide the same information about your own preferences.

Perspective change *mindfucks* are any *mindfucks* that involve an intentional alteration of someone's perspective. This might also be described as a framing exercise. When we use the term framing it is meant in the psychological sense. For example, when we say, "Let's play a game," we frame an experience in the context of a game. Alternatively, we might say "Okay, next I'm going to interview you." Each of these offers an opportunity to take on a different perspective.

Degrading or Ennobling *mindfucks* are those that directly affect your partner's sense of station. Degrading and ennobling activities are those that change or appear to change our position in the world or social status. An example of an ennobling *mindfuck* is to treat your partner like royalty, while an example of a degrading *mindfuck* is to give them the worst job you can think of.

Humiliation *mindfucks* are any that cause extreme embarrassment. This is deeply personal to the bottom. Some activities that are humiliating to one bottom may not affect another bottom at all.

***

Figure 3. Devil Wearing the Tube Gag

Interlude #2 Devil's Tube Gag

I recall fondly of a time when I was playing with a person at a small private party, who liked to be called "Devil" (pronouns are They/Them). Their primary partner was also at the event along with twenty or so people. We began to play and I fitted them with an open tube gag (also called a piss hole gag). It was essentially a stiff rubber tube about the width of a walnut strapped to their mouth. They could talk, but without the use of their lips and a severely restricted use of their tongue, it was quite difficult. Additionally, the gag made it very difficult to hold the drool in their mouth since they could only close their lips around the shaft of the stiff rubber tube.

Devil knelt in a squat at my feet as I sat in a chair. "State your name" I said, to which they mumbled "Asshole." "So, your name is Asshole?" I said "I think you've just given yourself a new nickname. What are you here for, Asshole?" I asked. They doubled over in laughter and embarrassment. When they regained composure, they sat back up onto their heels and mumbled something incoherent. Their eyes traced down to the already burning cigar nestled between my fingers.

I asked "What do you want with it?" At this point they knew that trying to talk was pointless so they rolled up their sleeve to reveal the halfway healed burns from a week or two before. "Right on the same spot?" I asked. "Uh huh" they said.

They wanted to be burned by my cigar, an extreme form of cigar play. We had done it before, and we both had a good time. They wanted to do it again. I could have just said yes, because I was amenable and they were enthusiastic about their interest. But I also knew that they were open to *mindfucking* and humiliation play, so I thought I would make it more difficult for them.

At the party there were two groups of people, Devil and myself in the back yard with a few others, and a large group inside playing board games. Among the group inside was Devil's primary partner. I told Devil to go ask their partner if it was okay to do cigar play today. So, they had to interrupt ten or so people playing a board game. They stammered to their partner through the gag without the use of their lips. What is more, as they struggled to speak a volume of spit began to drip from the gag. After several failed attempts to communicate with their restricted ability to speak, they got a notepad to write the question. This was a humiliation type *mindfuck* and was quite a show for the party guests.

***

One Size Does Not Fit All

Any of the suggestions on how to execute a *mindfuck* in this book are only as good as your knowledge of your partner. While it is true that some can become very adept at the cold read and use *mindfucks* that are likely to work on most people, knowing your bottom is the single most important aspect of *mindfucking*. If you do not know your partner well and try some of these tactics, you are likely to miss your mark. Doing this is like having a skeleton key and trying to filet a fish with it. Use the right tool for the right job. If you don't understand the job then my giving you the tools is not likely to help. If, on the other hand, you do the work to learn about your partner, then these tools may serve you well.

***

The History of *Mindfucking*

When we compile the practices of *mindfucking* it becomes clear that there are a wide variety of activities being lumped together. Because of this, it would be impossible to set a mark on a timeline and say that this is where the activity began. Certainly, we can track the development of our modern concept of consent to Wilhelm Reich and the sex positive movement in the 1920's. The sex positive movement gained significant substance with the women's liberation movement in the 1960's. We can also credit Lois Pineau for making the argument that we should move towards "active consent" as opposed to "passive consent" which has long been the norm in many cultures. We can also credit the organization Planned Parenthood for developing and promoting the F.R.I.E.S. acronym for consent. F.R.I.E.S. will be explained in detail later in the "Differentiating BDSM and Abuse" part of Section 2 (page 37).

Those tics on the timeline, however, are specific to the development of consent. A separate timeline (albeit a more complicated one) could be generated to chart the progress of modern ethics. These events would be relevant but would still fall short of answering the question "When did *mindfucking* start?" This is a very difficult question to answer completely but I can shed some light on things which helped it develop into what we know today.

Modern psychology can be traced back to the 1800s. Our modern understanding of the mind is heavily influenced by this field. Any kinkster will tell you that any tool, given considerable imagination, can be used in some sort of sexual way. So too, the tools of modern psychology can be utilized in a sexual way. Any form of manipulation can be retooled to be part of *mindfucking*. These scientists, though, did not invent the discourse of the human mind, they merely categorized it and measured it. Gaslighting was not a practice invented by modern psychologists but simply named by them.

I like to imagine that the 4' stone dildos that they sell at the gift shops outside of modern day Pompei are historically accurate reproductions of artifacts that were kept in the ornate brothels of the ash preserved city. The sex workers may have kept them as threats for the more unruly patrons. Similarly, I like to imagine ancient Egyptians donning headdresses fashioned like the pharaohs just for fun in the bedroom.

So, if it was happening before, then when did it start? In this book we cast a wide net in describing *mindfucking*. I would argue with that such a wide net, we are describing activities that are innately human. Surely, any culture would find space for a behavior like playing with someone's expectations, or role-playing a position of authority. As wide as our net is, we are using the caveats of ethical and consensual which can make our original question easier to answer.

For a *mindfuck* to be both ethical and consensual as we know them today, requires the modern concepts of ethics and consent. This drastically narrows our search from the whole of human history to only the last hundred years or so. Though we cannot easily attribute the practice to a specific date or person, we can make some educated guesses. The development of a cultural practice necessitates a culture. Though we can identify practices which we would today consider BDSM as far back as the rituals surrounding goddess Inanna in ancient Mesopotamia, tracing back the roots of our current BDSM culture goes much less far back. We can track the roots of our current fetish culture in America to a period just after WW2 where the gay community gave birth to a subculture known as the Leather Community. One might argue too that the culture was preceded by Victorian era fetish photography, or the Weimar republic in Germany. There are certainly earlier examples of fetishism such as in Figure 4 or even the writings of Marquis De Sade but a substantial record of an associated community is difficult to find.

Likely the first traceable use of *mindfucking* is the practice of degradation. Degradation and humiliation are fetish practices that are very popular and seem to emerge naturally as things that some people gravitate towards. Figure 4 on page 36 is an example of piss play from circa 1900 which might very well have been humiliation play.

The word mindfuck itself may have been coined but was certainly popularized by the authors Robert Joseph Shea and Robert Anton Wilson in their 1975 science fantasy trilogy *Illuminatus!* In the books, "Project Mindfuck" is an effort to create chaos and confusion as part of the fictitious religion discordianism. It gained popularity from there and now is in common use to describe anything that is confusing, disorientating, misleading, puzzling, or even enlightening.

By the popular definition, certainly what was described in the opening quote by Sun Tzu in "The Art of War" constitutes a mindfuck. McGinn, in his book simply titled "Mindfucking" suggests that the earliest record of the practice comes from Ancient Greece. Of the Sophists, he said "Their aim was not to argue for the truth, using only valid arguments and true premises; they felt free to win assent by any means possible, using rhetorical tricks, attractive fallacies, appeals to sympathetic emotion, fear, prejudice and all the rest." He continued to say "They resorted to psychological manipulation. They cajoled and seduced, messed with the minds of their audience, and had no compunction about the use of fallacies and falsehoods."

All of this, without alteration, could be used to describe our modern lawyers and many politicians. It is important to remember that, although these two examples of mindfucks in time bear the weight of the common definition of mindfuck, they are excluded from ethical, consensual and erotic *mindfucking* as we describe it. So, in summation, the modern practice of *mindfucking* likely came from either mid 1900s in America or earlier in the century in post WW1 Germany.

This may not be a satisfying explanation. To those that are dissatisfied with the explanation I can provide, I will let you know it is not going to be any better than that, at least not here. Sadomasochistic practices are often left out of history books or besmirched by the conservative elites. We must do what we can with what we have to understand our history.

***

Figure 4. Vintage Fetish Photography from Circa 1900

Differentiating BDSM and Abuse

The key difference between BDSM and abuse is negotiation, consent, and aftercare. One could also argue that another key difference is "power *with*" verse "power *over*." A BDSM experience should be empowering for all parties involved as opposed to empowering one party at the expense of the other. For more thorough explanation of power over verse power with, see "Section 4, Safety and Ethics" on page 69.

The importance of negotiation and consent cannot be overstated. Consent is best defined, in my opinion, by the F.R.I.E.S. acronym. Coined by Planned Parenthood, F.R.I.E.S. stands for Freely given, Reversible, Informed, Enthusiastic, and Specific. In the context of a *mindfuck*, this means getting consent when not role-playing or scening and respecting safe words during the *mindfuck* no matter what is happening. It also means informing your partner about the illusions or tricks you plan to play, ensuring that your partner is genuinely excited for the experience and not participating with ambivalence, hesitation, or some sort of obligation. Lastly, it means showing you respect the bounds of what has been consented to and not taking things any farther than has been previously agreed to. I will state this again in case you didn't hear me, *Steve*!

Freely given - Consent to be *mindfucked* should not be coerced. This means not asking a bottom for consent to be *mindfucked* while they are being interrogated, tortured, played with, pleasured, under the influence of any substance, or in an altered state of mind. If a bottom expresses interest in any of the above-mentioned conditions, be sure to check in and get consent when they are level headed and not distracted.

Reversible - Consent in a *mindfuck* can be withdrawn at any time. Safe words are a great tool for reversing consent when role-playing because traditional words used to reverse consent may be misinterpreted as part of the role-play. If for example, in a particular scene you might want to scream "NO, STOP, DON'T" even though you are having a good time and want it to continue. You can use a safe word to let your partner know that you really do want to stop.

Informed - Consent to a *mindfuck* requires that the person consenting is aware of everything to which they have consented. It may be a shock to you that this is a point of contention for many. I hear things like "If I ask permission, it will ruin the surprise." However, this is not true. There are strategies like spamming and long-term planning which can be employed while still informing your partner completely. Spamming and other strategies are explained in detail in the Section 5 on page 88.

Enthusiastic - Consent to a *mindfuck* must be enthusiastic. Even if you get a yes but it is an "Ok fine" or an "I guess so," there is clearly ambivalence there. It is far better to understand the source of ambivalence before an experience than it is to find out during or after.

Specific - Consent to be *Mindfucked* must be specific. For the same reason I receive resistance in the classroom on the point of informed consent, I have received resistance on this point as well. For those that feel like getting specific consent takes away from the potency of a *mindfuck*, I will recommend you look at Section 5, specifically negotiating a *mindfuck* on page 88. In the case of a *mindfuck*, specific consent means not introducing new activities or escalating mid scene if the activity had not already been agreed to. An example of this would be if you had agreed on degradation play, it is not appropriate to start humiliating them also just because they are often considered similar activities.

***

Interlude #3 Lex's Phone a Friend

A friend named Lex was bottoming in a scene with a fellow professional BDSM player. She was bound tightly to a spanking bench that exposed her ass and fixed her legs widely apart. After some light impact, he grabbed his phone and called a friend. "You wouldn't believe what I got right in front of me," he said to the friend on the phone, "This fox is all tied up bent over this bench at the dungeon, spread and dripping with anticipation." "Who the fuck is that?" shouted Lex. He continued, "Yeah of course you can come through! You know I like sloppy seconds anyhow. You bet you can bring the rest of the guys! Let's run a train like the good old days," he said with a chuckle. "See you in 15 minutes buddy," he said, hanging up the phone.

Her mind went wild with anticipation and speculation. "Who are these men? If they showed would I object or would I let it happen? He has got to be fucking with me! What if he isn't? Could I wriggle free of these ropes if I wanted to?" Her mind raced, until after what seemed like an eternity, he leaned in and whispered in her ear "You know I'm just fucking with you right?" A wave of relief swept over her still bound body, followed by a little disappointment and finally playful anger. "You dick" she lashed out while laughing.

This is an example of expectation *mindfuck* and possibly an illusion *mindfuck*. It was an expectation type of *mindfuck* because she began to expect that his friends were on their way. It would have been an illusion *mindfuck* if he was not on the phone at all for example.

***

Common Practice

If you ever have messed with your partner's head then you might have been *mindfucking* them. If you ever toyed with your partner's expectations or perceptions of reality in a way that was hot for both of you, then you might have been *mindfucking* all along.

The most common *mindfuck* seems to be the one of building anticipation and playing with expectations. You might say to your partner "I've got a special surprise for you when you get home" or "You are in for it when we meet up later." These glib threats or allusion to later activity are a kind of *mindfuck* and when done properly can get blood pumping in all the right places long before you even touch your partner.

For those that play with discipline, a common tool is the fictional infraction like "I know what you did and I'm disappointed. Confess or the punishment will be much worse." In this case the bottom is left to question their actions, going over what was said and done in their head searching for an answer. They might have even been hiding something that they become compelled to divulge so be prepared for a surprise confession if you press them hard.

***

Mindfucking in Dominance and Submission

Dominance and submission or simply D/s is the practice of engaging in mindful power exchange. This could be as simple as "For the next hour I am in charge of what we do" or as complicated as "for the duration of our relationship you must ask me before spending any money." For the sake of simplicity, we will be considering D/s as it applies to a specific scene such as an hour-long play session.

There are subtle things that happen all the time that create real or perceived power discrepancies in everyday life. Examples of this every day power imbalance are boss/employee, teacher/student, older/younger sibling, upper and lower classman, and so on.

By engaging in these intentionally, we can establish or reinforce a D/s dynamic. An example of this is making someone wait. If at the beginning of the scene you first get your partner into a submissive position such that they might think you are ready to begin, then you take a few minutes laying out all the toys you plan to use in a meticulous order, your partner may be made to think your time is more valuable than theirs since it seems like you are wasting their time. The same tactic can be used when you are meeting someone and you are late. This can backfire quite easily if the person decides they are tired of waiting or gets bored.

Perceived Power *mindfucks* are great for Dominance and submission. Role-play is a good example of this, which is covered in the *Mindfucks* in role-play on page 48. Another example of the perceived power *mindfuck* is power of the written word.

There cannot be an overstatement of the power of the written word. In our society, so much comes in writing that is official and presumed to be permanent or unyielding. The written word can be used in many ways to *mindfuck* your partner. First, I love to use a notebook in negotiation, it helps me remember exactly what has been said and the effect it has on someone else is significant. When I write what you say to me, you are being told without words that I will be holding you accountable. I am paying attention and what you say is on record. This *mindfuck* is used to great effect in "Interlude #4 The Power of the Written Word."

Another way to use the written word for *mindfucking* is with written consent forms, surveys, or "official rules." These might be things that you could just say to the person, but when they see it in writing they know that it's real. You could even invoke symbols like crests, seals or sigils to make your paperwork seem even more substantial. Lastly, I appear to have the power when I retain the paperwork, as the document can be a symbol of what was agreed upon.

Another approach for considering the role that *Mindfucking* can play in D/s is to use the example of a game. For the first example we can use a card game. A card game can be used to confuse the position of power with chance (An example of perceived power *mindfuck*). This is great for any couple but especially couples that are both submissive but will alternate topping. Neither one wants to dominate the play time so they can rely on the result of a card game to decide who will top or even what is to be done during the topping.

Alternatively, a D-type can use a card game as a way to conceal or confuse how much power they have in the situation. This can be done by creating the illusion of chance or putting an undue weight on chance as it relates to the outcome of a situation. We can let the cards decide when in reality we are making the decision on our own and creating a small chance, if any, that the cards will indicate anything different.

In "Section 5, Doing The Thing" there is an example of how Blackjack can be utilized for a *mindfuck* (page 102). There is an option for one-on-one play, and large group play. You can use a similar method to adapt nearly any card game.

***

Interlude #4 Power of the Written Word

It was evening at the North Hollywood Diner as the orange light of the setting summer sun shone through the stained-glass depictions of woodland animals in the windows. The diner was filled with wooden furniture, and the walls were lined with signed black and white photos with movie stars that had come to eat there before. This was a favorite spot for sadomasochists too because it was very close to the Threshold Society club house.

I was already sitting at a booth in a three-piece suit when she walked in. Her name was Mary, she stood six feet tall with skin as dark as a plum and curves just as voluptuous. She was my date for a dungeon party that had not started yet. We had agreed to sit down for a bite and negotiate before playing at the party.

Before she sat down, she threw down the manila envelope she held under her arm. It was heavy and the abruptness with which she tossed it suggested that she was a bit indignant even though she had complied. What she had complied with was my request to fill out a 35-page BDSM survey she clearly felt she should not have had to do.

As she sat down, Mary's head tilted to the side slightly as I opened the desk journal that I carried in my toy bag. It had a black leather binding and gilded pages. It was clear she had not expected the conversation to be so "official." At first, I looked through her survey, circling items and taking notes in my journal. Then, we talked about what she would like to do and what she was curious about. I took my notes on everything she said.

After some time, I proposed that we do some impact play and try out the taser before possibly incorporating it in the scene as well. She was open to being sexual and we discussed what that meant to her and how far I was personally willing to go in that arena at the time. After we reached an agreement, I turned the journal around and slid it across the booth to her, handing over the pen. "I need you to sign off in the notebook about what we agreed to" I said. After a pause, she asked me "Do I really have to?" Without a visible reaction I responded "Only if you want to play." She chuckled a bit but signed her name just as our food came to the table.

The *mindfuck* here is potentially not obvious. The first use of *mindfucking* was the survey. I could have prepared her emotionally and let her know it was long but I didn't. I wanted to see how she would react, what emotions would she have. Would she refuse, would she bargain, or maybe do a poor job just to get it over with?

Next with the use of my notebook, she was made to feel that I was attentive and that I planned to hold her accountable for what she said at the table. When I asked her to sign the negotiation, she may have felt a weight, again being reminded that she would be held to her word. Signing something makes us feel committed to it. Signing something can also remind us of times when we felt taken advantage of by banks, lawyers, police, or other people wielding power over us. I would call this a perceived power *mindfuck* because both the survey and the book serve to create the sense that our conversation was official and somehow bore more weight than any regular verbal agreement. This could have easily also been an illusion if I had a friend of mine pretend to be a notary or used an official seal or crest on the paperwork.

***

Figure 5. Role-Playing

Mindfucking in Role-Play

Role-play is a fantastic opportunity for *mindfucking*. An example might be taking on the role of a doctor and patient, or prison guard and prisoner. In both cases the D-type is playing the role of the person in the position of power and the s-type is playing the role of the person without power or with less power. Costumes can help the effectiveness of role-play as well. These are examples of the perceived power type of *mindfuck*. Simply by wearing a lab coat and hospital gown or a guard uniform and prisoner jumpsuit the desired power dynamic is reinforced.

Another *mindfucking* role-play opportunity to use *mindfucking* is to use ennobling type *mindfucking*. For example, one might enjoy treating their partner like a Queen. You can proclaim that it is Queen's day, and the day becomes focused on caring for her and serving her. This is particularly effective for those that have service as a love language. The Queen gets permission to be greedy and demanding and the servant (or even King) gets to focus on caring for their partner. For me, this is an excellent strategy because it is not typical or congruent with the dynamic that I usually maintain.

Yet another example of a *mindfuck* to reinforce or establish a power dynamic is to utilize the perceived power *mindfuck*. This could look like telling your partner that you have magic powers such as telepathy or telekinesis. I might tell my partner that I have placed them in invisible handcuffs that they cannot break free from. I could also tell my partner that I have penetrated their mind to extract their most guarded desires and sexual fantasies (this one works best if you have done your homework).

There are many advantages to this practice. Perhaps the D-type is in a bad habit of asking for feedback in the middle of the scene and killing the mood. To use a previous example, maybe the doctor/patient role-play is specifying that the patient is mute. Perhaps the D-type has a nasty habit of being too delicate with the s-type and role-playing a prison guard can help them get out of that headspace for the evening. Perhaps the s-type is not in the habit of serving the D-type and the Queen and servant role-play can be a way to get into a service role without feeling degraded (it is after all a privilege to serve the Queen).

What these all have in common is that they imply or overtly state that the D-type has power over the s-type. This can reinforce or establish a power exchange dynamic. The *mindfuck* in BDSM is power-with but can look like power-over. "Section 4," specifically page 76, we discuss the difference between the two in more detail.

***

Interlude #5 Truth Serum

The placebo effect can be a powerful tool. As part of an interrogation scene, one dominant told the story of how he wanted to create the illusion that he had administered a "truth serum" to the subject. He explained that he got consent from his bottom to administer a truth serum, *sodium thiopental,* for the sake of the interrogation. The bottom was informed that to help the "truth serum" work faster, niacin would also be administered. He advised the bottom that the side effects of the "truth serum" would include a sensation of body heat, flushing of the skin, dizziness, and itchiness.

Instead, the bottom was only given two pills of niacin (from different manufacturers, so they looked different). Niacin, or Vitamin B3, is an essential vitamin, available off-the-shelf in the vitamins/supplements section of almost any health food store or pharmacy. Large amounts of Niacin (1000 Mg or greater) should never be taken without consulting a doctor, as overdoses of this vitamin can lead to serious complications including liver damage. However, in recommended over-the-counter dosages (one or two 100-300 mg pills), the vitamin's side effects may include the very sensations of heating, flushing, dizziness, and itching that the interrogator suggested would be caused by the "truth serum."

Of course, no "truth serum" was ever administered, only niacin, and the side effects were carefully explained to the bottom. However, the result of using niacin to create tangible sensations created or amplified any placebo effects of taking the pill, assumed by the bottom to be attributable to the "truth serum" rather than the simple vitamin. In this case, this physically-reinforced placebo effect led the interrogation subject to believe the "truth serum" was working, and thus compelled them to be uncharacteristically honest and forthcoming with the requested secrets.

Through this strategy, the bottom has given consent that is informed and specific. The interrogator got consent to administer two substances but only administered one. There is no ethical conflict when getting consent for doing something and not doing it. The principal *mindfuck* here is that the side effects of niacin are misattributed to the (non-existent) truth serum, making the illusion feel real, even more so than if just imagined.

This is an example of both an illusion and perceived power type of *mindfuck*. The illusion is that the sensations are caused by the truth serum. It is also a perceived power *mindfuck* because the bottom holds the impression that the truth serum has given the interrogator more power than they actually did.

***

Mindfucking for Sadists

The sexual sadist is one who derives sexual pleasure from the pain, distress, or discomfort of their partner(s). *Mindfucking* is a valuable tool for those that do any kind of psychological sadism play. The goal can be to make your partner squirm, give that jolt of adrenaline that comes from a moment of real fear or just to leave your partner with a feeling of hot helplessness.

Degrading and Humiliating *mindfucks* can be utilized by the sexual sadist because just as the masochist may find humiliation and degradation erotic, so to the sadist can enjoy watching them suffer through it.

Asymmetric *mindfucks* can be used to torture bottoms. With the use of the "Wouldn't you like to know" attitude, they may be driven to greater and greater anticipation. You could even play 20 questions, giving them a chance to feel like they might get it out of you, but be tight lipped and give no useful hints to draw out the tension.

A great way to responsibly utilize this is to allow your partner to be under the illusion that they are in a greater amount of danger than they are. This not only accomplishes the desired feeling of a great thrill but also does so while taking a reduced risk. Maybe this is getting your partner with a fear of heights to jump from "high up" when in fact they are standing on a platform that is inches above the ground. Maybe it is, as we will see in the next interlude, the use of an object that feels like a knife but is actually dull.

***

Interlude #6 Midori's Argument with the Dungeon Monitor

This *mindfuck* was performed in a dungeon space during a party. Midori, a well-known kink educator and artist, was playing with a woman called Candy. Candy sat in an old wooden chair, the kind with ornate wood work on the armrests and back. First, Midori used rope to bind her to the chair, she bound her legs, she bound her arms, and she bound her torso all to the chair in which she sat. Next Candy was blindfolded.

Midori had put a lot of planning into this scene and had recruited several other partygoers to participate. They each grabbed a leg of the chair and hoisted her up high into the air. This is, as Midori explained, still a rope suspension. This reminds me of the litter, a hand-held carriage popular before motorized vehicles. Every so often while parading Candy through the dungeon, they would tip her to one side giving her the sensation that she was about to fall, all while being in the capable hands of her litter bearers.

Once Candy was placed back on the floor in her chair, Midori pulled out her knife. The knife clicked open and Candy shivered with excitement. The dungeon monitor interrupted Midori and they proceeded to argue. Knives, it seemed, were not allowed at the dungeon and the dungeon monitor wasn't having it. They proceeded to argue loudly while Candy stayed tied up in her chair. The dungeon monitor stormed off and Midori turned back to Candy and said "Screw him, I'm doing it anyway." The crowd gasped as Candy felt the blade on her skin.

In reality, the argument had been prearranged and the knife had only been real at first so that the sound of the knife unfolding was authentic. After that, it was just a piece of plastic that felt like an edge. The gasping crowd were all the same people Midori had recruited to carry Candy around.

After all was said and done, the binds came off and so did the blindfold. Midori revealed that she was using a piece of plastic and Candy got to meet the DM that was in on it the whole time.

This is an example of an asymmetric information, expectation and illusion *mindfuck*. It was a *mindfuck* of expectations when the chair was lifted and tilted with Candy still in it because she expected to fall. It was an asymmetric information *mindfuck* because Candy didn't know that the argument had been prearranged. Lastly it was an illusion mindfuck because given the context of the situation and all the information Candy had at that point, she had the illusion that the plastic piece being raked over her body was actually a blade and that Midori was going against house rules.

Section 3

Unethical, Non-consensual, and Unerotic Mindfucking

Mindfuck vs. *Mindfuck*

Much like the word fuck has as its non-consensual equivalent of rape, we could very well replace the word mindfuck as it refers to the unethical, non-consensual, or unerotic with mindrape as is suggested in the book "Mindfucking" by McGinn. I will refrain from this because I find the word rape repugnant and I expect it would turn some readers away from the text for that same reason. Instead, I will leave mindfuck the way it is and change the consensual, ethical, and erotic mindfuck to *mindfuck* with italics. So, from this point on, any time the word mindfuck is not italicized, it is meant as it used outside of the BDSM subculture.

We will explore mindfucking in detail here even though it is not per se the subject of this book. The reason for this is that when we indulge in BDSM activities, it can often look like abuse, and it becomes that much more important that we are adept at understanding the difference between BDSM and abuse. Additionally, mindfucking is a corrosive but typically socially acceptable activity often used to control people in one way or another. I believe that to be completely healthy *mindfuckers* we must be free from or at the very least aware of the mindfucking that is happening in our lives without ethics, without consent, and without eroticism.

***

Mindfucking in Accademia

In McGinn's book about the subject, he seeks to establish the philosophical significance of the mindfuck. I do believe he did his job in setting it aside from lying and bullshit. "The mindfucker is concerned with the listener's emotions." and later "The mindfucker aims at the psyche as a whole, while the liar and the bullshitter are content to focus on the belief component of the psyche." The author does explore the possibility of enjoyable mindfucks such as those in films like "Fight Club", "Sixth Sense", "The Usual Suspects", "Mulholland Drive", and "The Crying Game." He has, however, merely scratched the surface on the potential pleasure of *mindfucking*. He also explores what he calls a "positive mindfuck" such as how you might react when you learn some valuable new piece of information that changes your outlook on the world.

    McGinn does almost begin to understand our use of the word when he states "in some uses of the word, mindfucking is what happens in a certain kind of romantic encounter, when the other person somehow operates pleasurably on the mind to produce a welcome reaction." However, the mark is sorely missed when instead of investigating the practice of erotic *mindfucking* he goes on to ask "Weather all romantic love is a species of mindfucking." In my opinion, this proves to be the weakest component of his text and ultimately undermines the value of his other assertions.

    McGinn illustrates that the mindfuck is an endeavor to manipulate a person's or group of people's emotions. My favorite example

McGinn makes of a mindfuck is in Shakespeare's play Othello. In the play, Iago, angry that he has been passed over for a promotion, seeks to eliminate Othello from his station. Iago mindfucks Othello into a fit of jealous rage over his wife's perceived infidelity so powerfully that Othello kills his wife and later himself. In this way you can see that a single well executed mindfuck can lead to a set of ruined lives.

    In a scholarly journal article written in the South African Journal of Philosophy (2014, 33(1): 35-46) Kai Horsthemke explores the concept in the context of South African Apartheid. She aptly uses the example of the education system in South Africa in the late 1950's. Hendrick Verwoerd who was an Assembly member at the time, and was also the designer of an intentionally inferior education system for non-whites (later referred to as Bantu) in South Africa, was quoted saying the following in the June 15th, 1959 House of Assembly meeting. "Education must train and teach people in accordance to their opportunities and life according to the sphere in which they live... Native education should be controlled in such a way that it is in accordance with the policy of the state... Racial relations cannot improve if the result is the creation of a frustrated people." Later he was quoted saying "Until now he (the Bantu pupil) has been subject to a school system which withdrew him away from his community and misled him by showing him the Green Pastures of European society in which he was not able to graze... What is the use of teaching the Bantu child mathematics when it cannot use it in practice?" If the spirit of these words is still unclear, a statement of the minister of Bantu education made almost a decade later spells it out exactly "The money being spent on Bantu education is not being spent out of love for the Bantu but for the future of the whites."

***

Mindfucking in Politics

Politicians are almost universally involved in mindfucking. Each politician is required to gain popularity against his or her opponent, when they use effective but underhanded and manipulative tactics, they win and perpetuate the cycle. More than just individual politicians, governments mindfuck their own citizens to create a climate where their atrocities are seen as justified or normal day to day activity.

Not surprisingly, most governments will effectively gaslight their own people into thinking that they do not do this. It is easy, for example, for Americans to look into the history books and see how in the 1940's Nazi's use of internment camps, slave labor, forced sterilization, propaganda, and mass murder were unethical. It seems to be much more challenging for those same Americans to see how in the year 2020 immigrant children were being separated from their families and "lost," or how infants have died in ICE custody, or how women in these detention camps are being forced to be sterilized, or the forced sterilization of Native American women. For more information on the ways that the American People have been systematically mindfucked I would recommend "A People's History of the United States" by Howard Zinn.

Arguably the most egregious example of mindfucking in modern politics, at least within American borders, is how Trump intentionally downplayed the seriousness of the Covid-19 pandemic. Because of his blatant manipulation of the American public, 2020 was the most fatal year for American citizens in history. The reason this was a mindfuck is because the lie was perpetrated specifically to manipulate the emotions of the American people, as Trump would later admit on a phone call with a man named Woodward. Trump was quoted in a Feb 26th press briefing as saying "Wash your hands, stay clean. You don't have to necessarily grab every handrail unless you have to," he said, the room chuckling. "I mean, view this the same as the flu." Later in March 19th in a private interview he was quoted saying "To be honest with you, I wanted to always play it down. I still like playing it down. Because I don't want to create a panic." This mindfuck contributed to more than half a million deaths from Covid-19 by March 2021.

***

Mindfucking for the Political Underdog

On the flip side of the coin groups without massive funding from corporate or national interests can use mindfucking in political activism. George Orwell once wrote "every joke is a tiny revolution." The absurdism of Mathew Silver as he posts up in New York's public spaces in a small one-piece swimsuit making farts and shouting about the power of love also comes to mind immediately. His absurdist approach to activism and street performing causes people to be mindfucked in the most benevolent way, one that leads to love and understanding. In a rare moment, as part of the "Stand Up For Passion" series, when Mathew Silver was on camera but not so much in character, in a video as part of the Stand Up For Passion series, he said: "I want to see the global heart awakened."

Another example is the Barbie Liberation Organization which in the early 1990's switched hundreds of Barbie's voice boxes with G.I. Joe's. The Barbie's now said "Dead men tell no lies," in a gruff voice, while the G.I. Joe's now said "I love to go shopping with you," in a light bubbly voice. This was meant to inspire a deeper conversation about gender roles.

***

Mindfucking in corporate culture

Corporate culture is no stranger to a good old fashioned mindfuck. In corporate culture it is commonplace to take advantage of customers or even employees in a way that we would consider unethical and non-consensual.

The purpose is usually to save or make more money or to gain control over another person. An employee might for example be made to feel unimportant before negotiating a salary adjustment. This would lead to the employee being less aggressive or assertive during negotiation. This can be accomplished by the boss scheduling a meeting with the employee then repeatedly rescheduling. Another example is leaving a component of the compensation plan out and not mentioning it so that the employee needs to fight for a basic component instead of something extra.

Another good example is the "We are a family here" tactic. With this tactic companies will give employees the impression that "we are just one big family," and I suppose they are not wrong since often families are abusive. They will take advantage of your willingness to go above and beyond for "family" asking you to do more than you are being paid to do. What is worse, the "family atmosphere" is billed as a benefit and used as an excuse why other benefits are less robust. It is also done to obscure the hierarchy when management tries to give their workers the sense that they are all in it together.

***

Mindfucking in Sales and Marketing

   Mindfucking occurs often in advertising but again we must acknowledge that this mindfucking is the kind that occurs outside of the bounds of what we consider ethical and consensual mindfucking. Advertisers are constantly working to undermine your self-confidence, self-respect, sense of identity, sense of belonging, all while providing a solution to those issues in their product. In the most extreme cases advertisers will provide solutions to problems which do not actually exist. Douching is a pungent example of this manufacturing of an issue.

   For as long as humans have existed, their genitals have had an aroma. This changes over time and in accordance with health, diet, and other factors. Douching is a practice as old as time, once thought to prevent pregnancy. In the 1900's, however, as the science of contraception was developed further, empty promises of preventing pregnancy with *Lysol douching* were no longer credible. So instead of throwing in the towel, companies sowed insecurity among women about the odor & hygiene of their vaginas. A whole host of products marketed toward sanitizing and adding fragrance to vaginas are still available today. Even now as douching is clearly unhealthy, they are sold along with sprays and wipes geared to wipe away odor and the shameful feeling of the corporation's creation.

    I taught a Mindfuck class and taster, requiring all participants to sign a release form consenting to being *mindfucked* in the taster component. I laughed when some refused and were very vocal about not wanting to be *mindfucked*. "I hope you don't own a TV, Radio, or read anything ever," I thought to myself. As consumers we are constantly being exposed to mindfucks. You won't look cool unless you get these shoes. You won't be sexy unless you buy this car. You will never get a man with eyelashes as short as yours. You will never get the job of your dreams unless you go to this school. You can never maintain your health unless you get this juicer. The list goes on nearly to infinity.

Figure 6. 1970's Douche Ad

The basis of sales is insecurity. Secure people don't buy things they don't need. Magazines, radio shows, television shows, all seek to make you feel insecure about not having a product they benefit from you purchasing. Next time you watch an advertisement look for it. How is the ad stating or implying you will suffer, or are lesser, without their product?

It is important to consider what the long-term effect of these ads might be. What is the result of constantly being made to feel less than or insecure if you don't buy? Could they be undermining our self-confidence, sense of security, sense of self-worth on a global scale? Could society as a whole be affected by this practice? I am not going to answer these questions for you but I do feel like they are important questions to ask.

Salesmen are just as bad as the advertisers if not worse. They even categorize the mindfucks as sales techniques. Though there are many, two that come to mind are the "two options close" and the "take away close." With the two options close the salesman gives you two options, both options lead to the salesman getting what they want. "Well, do you suppose you will buy the monthly subscription at $9.99 per month or would you like to save some money and pay $99 for the whole year up front?" Both options are you making a purchase, and as a customer you don't feel manipulated because you feel you were given choices. I've even heard people say, don't use that more than twice in a conversation or the mark... er, I mean the customer will feel manipulated.

    The "take away close" is used when a customer feels apprehensive and the salesman begins to withdraw from the customer, causing them to advance. Maybe the salesman has samples out and starts to pack them up. Maybe the salesman says "Y'know, not everyone can handle the 90X model. Maybe it's not for you." By withdrawing, the customer is caused to feel a sense of urgency and reveal how attached they are to the product they have yet to buy. Then the salesman has the customer in the palm of his hand.

***

Section 4

Safety and Ethics

Cautions and warnings

Erotic *Mindfucking* is considered a form of edgeplay because it is capable of doing emotional or psychological damage in short order. What is more, the damage may not be obvious in the moment and could be unapparent even to the person receiving the *mindfuck* until much later. We must acknowledge before proceeding that, as with any form of psychological play, there are risks that are unknown even to the bottom themselves. As a result, we must be prepared for the possibility of mistakes or harm even when we take every measure to reduce the risks.

It is critical to have an action plan for what we are going to do if things don't go the way you have planned. Just like when practicing fire play or knife play, we should be prepared for handling cuts and burns, when we practice *mindfucking*, we must be prepared for a traumatic experience for either the top or the bottom. See "Section 4, Safety and Ethics," page 72, for more information on trauma awareness in *mindfucking*.

It may be easy to imagine a bottom being traumatized but it is also important to understand how a top can be traumatized. Let's imagine the scene gets very dark, and although the bottom feels comfortable with the scene, the top could be shocked about what the bottom is capable of receiving or even shocked about what they themselves are capable of dishing out. Perhaps they have the sensation that they have become a worse person for the experience or that they have opened Pandora's Box inside themselves. Tops can often experience self-doubt as a result of enjoying activities that "good people don't do" and require some reassurance from the bottom or friends. It is CRITICAL that a top be prepared and permitted to call a safe word and end the scene based on their own limits and experiences

***

Interlude #7 Monsignor Hollywood and the Shit Sack

At a *mindfuck* class I went to early in my discovery process, an instructor known as Monsignor Hollywood taught a class at the Threshold Society in Los Angeles, California. His class about *mindfucks* was riddled with examples, but the one that stuck with me the most was that he presented a bag whose content was heavy and wet. He asked some volunteers about their preferences. One volunteer said that they have a hard time with germs and messes. This was the volunteer he invited to reach into the bag and feel what was inside of it. She was apprehensive but he did not pressure her in the least. He said "All I can do is present you with an opportunity to confront that fear. Only you can take that opportunity."

She reached into the bag, and her face contorted with disgust but she persisted. He asked her to describe the sensation as she felt around in the bag. "It's wet, squishy, soft with little bits of hard things," she said wincing. "You are gonna want to wash your hands," he said to her as she pulled her hand from the bag, wet with who knows what. It was later revealed that the bag was filled with a strange assortment of snack food and liquids, made to simulate the sensation of a bag full of feces.

This was an illusion type *mindfuck* and also possibly a humiliating *mindfuck*. It was an illusion because the bottom was made to think that the sensations they were experiencing were from feces and not from snack foods. It was potentially a humiliating experience if the person bottoming would feel humiliated by the idea of touching shit in front of an audience.

***

Trauma Informed *Mindfucking*

You might ask yourself, "why would someone want to do this?" People are drawn to some things without knowing any type of explanation. For those people, I would say that acceptance is more important than explanation. If an explanation is important to you, by all means, seek it, but it should not serve as a pre-requisite to acceptance.

Other times people intentionally seek to fetishize things. They may feel controlled by their fears and aversions, and exploring them in a relatively safe environment gives them an opportunity to gain leverage over those sensations.

Eye Movement Desensitization and Reprocessing (EMDR) is a type of therapy that can be used to reduce the effect of trauma in our lives. With EMDR a participant may revisit a traumatic experience where they felt powerless. They can add in a token of power like a friend or an item, thereby empowering themselves in their own recollection of the experience. With BDSM we have the opportunity to do something very similar.

Instead of revisiting the memory as in EMDR, in BDSM we can relive the experience. Take for example someone who was traumatized by verbal abuse and spanking. In BDSM we can revisit the experience by having our partner yell at us and spank us. This time however, we are also experiencing the warm embrace of our lover, maybe some sexual touches, and patience and compassion if we experience some difficult emotions in the process. What is more, we could have our partner yell positive things like "YOU ARE SO BEAUTIFUL AND PRECIOUS TO ME! I'M LUCKY TO HAVE YOU IN MY LIFE!" This way those memories that trouble us are mixed around with memories of our partners being insightful, compassionate, patient, and caring.

 It is important to realize that even though we may have experienced trauma that may or may not impact our play preferences, some people are not interested or ready to confront it directly. It may not be a good idea for some people to EVER face their trauma through BDSM. This does not mean that playing at all is off limits, but it does mean that we may need to be aware of our partner's trauma or our own trauma.

***

Negotiating Trauma Informed Play

Here is a list of questions you might ask your partner in your preparation of an action plan.

- What happened the last time you were traumatized?
- What kind of care was required for you to feel safe after you were last traumatized?
- What is the plan if one of us becomes traumatized?
- Is it an automatic end of scene?
- Do you want to do a check in at that point?
- Do you want to push through it?
- What if I am not able or suitable to care for you when you are feeling traumatized?
- Is there a friend we can call?
- Do you have a therapist/psychiatrist that we can get in touch with if we need to?

***

Interlude #8 Sox Gets What's Coming to Her

This *mindfuck* happened during a party where I was working as an event organizer. My victim, er, I mean subject was the Head Dungeon Monitor we called Sox. She volunteered as many as 12 hours per week in support of the dungeon Sanctuary LAX Studios, that many of us consider our second home. You could never tell that she was volunteering because she took the job very seriously.

 At the onset of the party as Sox arrived, I asked her "can I have your consent to do some light *mindfucking* on you?" With a confused look on her face and hesitation, she said "Sure." To which I replied "Good, you are gonna get what you have coming to you tonight!" She was visibly puzzled. We did not have a play or sexual relationship so it was clearly not a threat of something we had never done before.

 Later in the evening, I would pull her aside as if to comment about some party goer I was concerned about and say "You are gonna get what you have coming to you." I even got some of the other Dungeon Monitors to say something like "Hey Sox, I heard you are gonna get what you have coming to you," as if everyone knew but her.

 After a fair amount of light psychological torment over the course of several hours, it was time to announce the winners of the prize drawing for the evening. While we were addressing the audience and had their full attention, I called Sox to the stage. I said "All night I have been telling you that you were gonna get what you had coming to you, and now it's happening, it's time to get it." Just then my partner handed me a rolling suitcase which I proceeded to unzip onstage in front of Sox. I continued to address her and the audience "We heard that someone stole your toy bag Sox. That sucks and I know that what we have put together is no replacement for what you lost but it's a bit of a head start to building back your collection. Each of the vendors here tonight has donated a little something and we have put in a number of items ourselves. We love you Sox. You really had this coming to you!"

This is an example of an expectation *mindfuck* because I gave Sox the impression that something bad was going to happen to her. It is also a use of the asymmetric information *mindfuck* because I was teasing her about something I knew that I also knew she didn't know.

***

Ethical Considerations

Berné Brown illustrates the difference between Power-over and Power-with quite eloquently in a document called "Dare to Lead." I find the distinction essential for fostering healthy power exchange relationships such as those that can be found in BDSM. When we engage in BDSM activities we ultimately empower all involved. This is an example of power-with behavior. Things that we do often feel or mimic power-over situations but are ultimately part of a fantasy. Take for example a prison guard and prisoner fantasy. The bottom might take great pleasure in the feeling of helplessness and freedom from decision making as a sexy helpless prisoner. Maybe the prisoner even solicits the guard, begging for the chance to trade sex for some comfort or dignity. We can play the game that the prison guard has power-over the bottom, but at the end of the scene, we step out of our role and care for our partners. In fact, the whole time you are doing that scene you are caring to observe your partners limits and preferences. No one truly had power-over the other in that example, even if it feels that way.

If at the end of the scene you or your partner refuse to let go of the roles they had taken on for role-play, if they refuse to let the illusion evaporate, or let the mystery be revealed then there is a significant problem.

It might be tempting when you are topping to let the illusions persist. You might want to let them continue to think that you have psychic powers, let them believe that you are holding the antidote to the "poison" they ingested earlier but that would be unethical. It is true, they gave you permission to fuck with their mind, but there are limits. One of the limits you as the top are OBLIGATED to observe is the temporal one. The scene must end at some point. Even if your partner forgot to mention when the scene should end, you are not free from this constraint. It is your responsibility as the top to call the scene at some point, even if your bottom doesn't. If the scene never ends, it's not BDSM, it's abuse and you're not a Dom, you're just an asshole.

If someone has not consented to be in your scene, then keep them out of it. This includes the practice of BDSM in public spaces. I would say this can be a difficult line to draw for some but it is something I am happy to make clear for you here. If the method of control, domination, stimulation is apparent and unusual to onlookers, then it can be considered obscene and a violation of the onlooker's consent. This distinction requires some cultural sensitivity. For example, if I train my submissive to feel degraded by the requirement that they hold my pinky finger as we walk, this is not sufficiently unusual as to be considered obscene. If on the other I have her on a leash and collar then that is sufficiently unusual to be considered obscene. Remember, it is not your measure of what is considered obscene that counts, but the observers. I would say that wearing a pup hood, which many people feel is appropriate in public, would be appropriate so long as it is not an excuse for obscene behavior. If your *mindfuck* is in public it is only ethical if it is undetectable by an uninformed onlooker.

    It is the top's responsibility to protect the bottom. This may mean that the top will have to refuse some activities that have been enthusiastically consented to if they are not confident and able to do those activities without harming the bottom. Sometimes even when the top has the ability to skillfully execute the activity it still might be a bad idea. For example, if the bottom is asking to be cut and scarred but the top does not think the bottom has put sufficient thought into the permanent marking, the top has the right to refuse to do it.

It is one thing to make a mistake about someone's limits but it is entirely different to know that the person you are playing with is unable to express their limits in the moment and proceed past them with full knowledge. The latter is not only immoral but it can also be criminal. To know you are exceeding someone's limits and proceeding simply because they are not able to object is tantamount to rape.

***

Interlude #9 Monsignor Hollywood and the Clairvoyant Insight

There were two young sisters that were always showing up to Monsignor Hollywood's classes with their mother. He said that the two of them definitely wanted to get fucked but he wasn't into it. He never flat out rejected them because he enjoyed the tension that it created.

He knew that these women would be showing up to his *mindfuck* class, so before the day of he reached out to one sister. "Tell me something about your sister. Tell me something that only you and your mother would know. "

During the class Monsignor Hollywood went on about his psychic ability. He looked straight at the other sister, the one whose secret had been revealed in private. He said "I'm getting something over here, you, does bitty mean anything to you?"

Bitty had been the name of the blanket that she carried around constantly as a child. She was very attached to it and kept it around longer than her family thought was appropriate. She had some shame attached to this experience because her cousins used to make fun of her for it and she certainly didn't tell people about it now.

The woman was embarrassed and bewildered. Her face flushed beat red and her eyes widened with shame and embarrassment. Suspicion grew inside her that her sister or her mother had sold her out. Or perhaps Monsignor Hollywood was psychic and had gleaned this information straight from the depths of her mind. In either case, she was deeply embarrassed and she averted her eyes.

This was an example of an asymmetric information *mindfuck* because the woman did not know if Monsignor Hollywood was psychic or if he had somehow learned it from a family member. It is also a perceived power *mindfuck* because the audience and the woman may think that he was able to read anyone's mind and that no thought was safe from his knowledge. Based on her reaction it was also a humiliation type *mindfuck*, because the deeply personal information revealed left her feeling extremely embarrassed.

***

Interlude #10 Midori's Chainsaw Scene

  This scene took place at a dungeon in an old foundry. They had a private rental of the space and had previously negotiated a fear play and CBT scene. The floor was concrete and the decor was industrial. David sat in a chair designed especially for genital torture so there was a conspicuous section missing in the middle of the seat. He was naked from the waist down, with a long plywood plank extended from underneath his bare ass to several feet in front of him. He was blindfolded and bound to the chair at the wrists and ankles.
  As David wondered what would happen first, the sound of a crank start of a two-stroke engine filled the air. Midori revved the engine and it was clear that she had a chainsaw in hand. Midori began to chop up the plank bit by bit, wood chips flying everywhere. Slowly, she cut pieces off, ever progressing towards David's exposed genitals, precariously sitting on the other end of the plank. The vibration grew ever more and more intensely as the chainsaw grew closer.
  Then, unknown to her blindfolded bottom, she switched to a different chainsaw whose chain had been removed. She used this new chainsaw and edged ever closer to his genitals. Then finally when she was about to hit him with the chainsaw, her assistant came in with a powerful wand vibrator and vibrated him at the moment it seemed he would be cut apart. The vibrations from the wand, the buildup of tension, the sensation of fear of

bodily harm, it all built for David and he came all over the saw dust covered floor. After the blind fold was removed and David found out what had actually happened, they all had a good laugh.

This is an example of an illusion mind fuck. David was given a lot of evidence that a working chainsaw was about to cut him. He had enough trust in his top that he knew he would be safe in his mind, but his body was getting a lot of messages otherwise. The sensation of fear was erotic for him. The vibrations of the chainsaw chewing through the wood and eventually the wand vibrator was enough to bring him to climax.

***

Therapeutic Potential

As a preface to this chapter, I must say that if you have significant trauma from which you or your partner suffer, then there is no replacement for counseling and/or therapy. BDSM practices can be therapeutic, but it's best to explore those aspects along with professional support.

Perhaps the reason why some people are attracted to *mindfucking* is because they experienced abuse from loved ones in a similar fashion. *Mindfucking* in a BDSM setting gives us the opportunity to experience familiar and attractive tropes that might usually be characteristic of a toxic or unhealthy relationship. This time, however, we can engage with a loving partner who is mindful of our limits and wellbeing.

In addition to healing that may come unintentionally from exploring things that are sexy, scary, or challenging to us, there is a distinct opportunity to mindfully engage with the intention of healing fears or traumas. As previously mentioned, there is a significant potential for re-traumatization or to exacerbate shame or fear, and for this reason this approach is not for everyone. I do feel that the potential is significant enough and its impact substantial enough that it merits discussion.

Traumatic experiences, for the sake of this text, will be defined as stressful experiences that negatively impact a person's life, long after the event. Examples of this might include someone who was in a car accident, feeling fear from being in a car or hearing sounds of a car. Another example might be a person who was bit by a dog and now fears all dogs, even the most docile and friendly. You could see how either of these experiences could get in the way of daily life.

By experiencing things that were traumatic at one point, we may be able to "rewrite the ending" or "say what we never got to say." We might be compelled to revisit traumatic experiences because having the experience in a "safe space" can lead to leverage over the original experience and the influence it has on our lives. Doing a *mindfuck* involving a car could be messing around in a car, or masturbating in the passenger seat while someone else is driving. A *mindfuck* involving a fear of dogs could be to have dog sound effects for use during play, or even role-playing as a dog.

We might, like with the "Interlude #11, Spider in a Jar" interlude on page 85, get an opportunity to face our fear. Queen Ana was able to experience her fear intimately and in a way that was relatively safe. She also got to blend that experience with feelings of being sexy and intimate with her partner. After it was over, she got to feel proud of herself for being brave and she knows that she can live through that fear. Today she still has a slight fear of spiders but it is a lot better than it was before.

With regard to rewriting the ending for past experiences, this is a great way to utilize role play of personal growth. We often feel stuck with feelings of regret when we had an interaction we wished had gone differently. With role-play we can revisit those experiences and give them the ending we wish we had in the first place, giving our minds an opportunity to experience the resolution we missed.

Often with traumatic experiences, we have the experience of freezing up. This is part of that stress response we have all experienced where we either fight, flee, or freeze. If you froze up in that traumatic experience it may be helpful to role-play. This time when you would have frozen, have a plan of action, do what you couldn't before. We are often left with feelings of regret that sound like "If I had only fought back." With BDSM we can explore what it might have been like to fight back.

It is important that our partners always have the chance to give informed consent, but this is especially true when we plan to act out some trauma we have experienced. This kind of work, often called shadow work, can be dark and heavy. Not every partner will have the emotional resilience or state of mind required for this work and it is essential they are given the chance to make that choice for themselves. If you want to explore consensual non-consent because it is a fantasy of yours, it is one thing, but it is an entirely different thing if you want to explore consensual non-consent to process your rape trauma. Both are valid but engaging in the latter without informing your partner is dishonest and unethical. You both may need special aftercare after such an emotionally heavy scene.

***

Interlude #11 Spider in a Jar

This is a *mindfuck* I enjoyed in private play with my slave wife Queen Ana. We often engage in fear play and this is an extreme instance of that. She has a fear of spiders that she was interested in gaining leverage over. Also, the both of us are well aware of the arousing potential of acute fear. I happen to live in an area that has black widow spiders, which would emerge at night from cracks and crevices in the garage woodwork to set up their webs for the evening.

I got her consent to have a spider, captured in a jar, for fear play as long as the jar remained closed and there was no risk of being envenomed. I brought the spider to the night stand as we did a bondage scene on the bed. After she was tied down, and blindfolded, I removed a second jar from within the nightstand. I had previously hidden second jar, which was entirely empty. This jar was placed on her bound naked body. Ever so slowly I unscrewed the jar, in a way that made a clear and recognizable sound. She panicked but did not call her safe word. As she struggled against her restraints, the jar, which was open and still on her body, fell over.

I shouted "Don't knock it over! It's going to get out!" This sent her into even more of a panic and she writhed and wriggled against her wrist and ankle cuffs. She worked herself into a sweat at this point.

I said firmly but calmly "Hold still so I can get it." She did her best to hold still, as she quietly shuttered with fear. I grabbed my whip and used the cracker, a strand of masonry twine, and gently ran it across her body. She was sure she felt the spider scurrying across her skin.

She panicked even more than before. Shrieking and screaming for her life. She finally called out "RED", her safe word, and I pulled up her blindfold. "Where is it?!" she said, still in a panic. I gestured silently to the spider still peacefully sitting in the jar on the nightstand. She looked at the empty jar on the bed and we both had a good laugh.

I would call this an illusion *mindfuck* because she was sure she could feel the spider on her body. My partner had the opportunity to experience terror in a safe space. Deep down she knows that I am very much concerned for her safety and would not put her in harm's way. In the moment she was sure that a dangerous venomous spider was crawling around on her naked body. Since playing this way, Ana has gained leverage over her fear of spiders. Recently she even captured a spider from inside the house and let it free outside without any help.

***

Section 5

Doing the Thing

Negotiating *Mindfucking*

As has been mentioned previously, negotiation is an essential precursor to any BDSM scene, *mindfucking* included.

If you are going to negotiate, you have to first get permission to negotiate. Those who do not and start negotiating with someone who they just met or who has never expressed interest, is revealing themselves as the least desirable kind of neophyte. Furthermore, a mistake many people tend to make even when they have some experience is asking if someone is interested in playing as opposed to asking if someone is interested in negotiating play. They may not be sure if they are willing to play, but they may still be willing to negotiate to see what you have to offer. The most effective strategy for asking someone if they want to negotiate is a strategy I call "The Conditional Ask with Explanation."

***

Conditional Ask with Explanation

In my experience this is the best way to proposition someone. It gets past the often unspoken "why" objection and also gives the person a way to say no if they are uncomfortable saying no. The structure of the conditional ask with explanation proposition is as follows: If X, then Y, because Z, where X is a condition, Y is a proposition, and Z is an explanation. An example of this is: If you are free later, I would love to negotiate a *mindfuck* scene with you, because I think we could have a lot of fun together. This gives the person receiving the proposition an easy way to say no.

You might think that encouraging them to say no is counterproductive but it isn't. Remember that F.R.I.E.S. acronym, we don't want an unenthusiastic yes. By giving a conditional statement at the beginning of a proposition, you give the person a way to decline which is pre-approved. Some people have trouble saying no, so if you say "if you are free later…" first, then they can say "sorry, I don't have the time."

Also, by saying "because…" you give a reason why you want to do the activity and get in front of an objective that might be unspoken "why though?" The person you are propositioning may question your intentions. "Sure, you want to play but *why* do you want to play with *me*?" By stating a reason, you take the time to address a common concern.

Another example of this would be "Hey Ana, if you feel ready to try it, I'd love to experiment with that new *mindfucking* technique we learned in Sir Ezra's book, because I always have fun when I play with you." Then Ana can say, "I'm not ready" without any trouble and it is easy for you to not take it personally. Also, if she is wondering why you want to try it, she knows it's because you always have fun when playing together.

***

Making Negotiation Sexy

A challenge I see many people face comes from the misconception that negotiation cannot be fun and sexy, when it absolutely can! I personally like to be affectionate and thrive on the tension often present in a negotiation. A good negotiation can take time and some people can become frustrated with excitement. Personally, I am always put at ease by the discomfort of others. I like to let my negotiating partner squirm with anticipation and impatience. It drives me to be more thorough and detailed in my process.

It may be appropriate to give the person a taste of what is to come during the negotiation. If you have an elaborate setting for a scene like a dungeon, consider negotiating at the dungeon. If you and your partner are expecting to do an interrogation scene, you can employ an interrogation style negotiation to tantalize them. These all have to be negotiated ahead of time but it could be as simple as, "how do you feel about doing our negotiation in the dungeon space?" You may get a no and I strongly suggest you take it and move on because your partner might feel that the setting is distracting or is concerned about not having their wits about them.

Negotiating *mindfucks* can be tricky if you are counting on some or all of it being a surprise. It is essential that negotiation take place before a *mindfucking* scene and the F.R.I.E.S. acronym states, among other things, that we must get "Specific and Informed consent." So how do we get specific and informed consent without ruining the surprises we have in store? It is a question that is invariably asked every time I teach this class in person. There are two solutions which can be used individually or in combination. They are long term planning and spamming. Both of these strategies utilize a feature of memory's limited ability to our advantage.

Long term planning allows you to negotiate far in advance. Everyone's memory is different but in general if you have a lengthy negotiation a few weeks ahead of time, the bottom will be less able to remember what they consented to. This is even more effective when you use a notebook and take notes. This way what they agreed to can be fresh in your mind and distant in theirs. There should, however, be some negotiation right before the event. Even if the negotiation right before is as simple as "how are you feeling about what we agreed to previously?" or "Are you ready to do the scene we discussed before?" Checking in right before a scene is strongly encouraged because you don't know what head space your partner is in unless you ask. Maybe what you discussed days before sounded great but today is just a bad day. Perhaps there was a near miss in traffic on the way to the location that left them feeling shaken. We cannot know if their headspace or stance on an activity has changed if we don't ask.

    Spamming, on the other hand, can be done right before play. You can get specific & informed consent and cause your partner to be unable to determine what consent they provided was pertinent. They will be likely to forget almost everything you discussed besides the first, last and most bizarre activities. Spamming can look like the following:

- Can I spank you?
- Can I flog you?
- Can I sit on your lap?
- Can I use the violet want on you?
- Can I leave you with bruises?
- Can I use my taser on you?
- Can I pull your hair?
- Can I do knife play?
- Can my friend Michael join us?
- Can I conduct an interrogation?
- Can we do chemical play?

- Are you open to penetration with toys?
- Are you open to penetration with my penis?
- Are you open to fluid exchange?
- Can we do fire play?
- Are you open to humiliation?
- Are you open to degradation?
- Are you open to sacrilege play?
- Can I spit in your mouth?
- Will you wear a rubber mask?
- Can we record this session?
- Can I slap you with a fish? (please note many of these questions would require follow up questions but those were not included for brevity)

Now let's imagine you get a positive response for every question. Are you going to do all those things in one scene? Probably not. Does the bottom have a clear idea of what you plan to do? Likely not. When I wrote this list of questions, I was imagining an electro-torture interrogation scene. Is that what you had pictured when you read the list of questions? Be sure not to ask the important questions first or last since the bottom is most likely to remember the first and last item in a list.

Because the mind is not able to remember everything, it tends to focus on the last thing mentioned in a list. The mind also may focus on the thing that seems to be different from the rest of the items in the list. This way you can get informed consent without leading your partner to knowing exactly what to expect.

It is important to remind you that we must act ethically and with the best interest of our partner in mind at all times. The two previously mentioned strategies, as with most of the content in the book, have the potential to be used in unethical ways. The point of the spamming and long-term planning strategies is not to take advantage of your partner but to provide something that your partner desires, including surprise and mystery.

***

Interlude # 12 Monsignor Hollywood and the Rubber Masks

Another *mindfuck* exemplified in a class by Monsignor Hollywood is the wearing of masks. It is a powerful mind fuck to play with identity using costumes and masks. In his class, he had three volunteers seated on stage facing the audience. He asked them to close their eyes as he reached into a bag with rubber masks in it. These were the type of masks you can get at a Halloween store that smell of rubber gloves and often don't sit tight against the face.

The first volunteer got a clown mask put on them, the second was a poodle, the last volunteer got a dolphin mask. The audience laughed and cheered with the addition of each of the three masks. None of the volunteers knew what mask they were wearing. This is a very dynamic *mindfuck*. Depending on the mask, who is wearing it, what is expected and whether or not the wearer is informed of the nature of the mask it could be expectation, perceived power, asymmetric information, perspective alteration, degrading, ennobling or humiliating type of *mindfuck*. I later asked Monsignor Hollywood what was meant by the specific masks. He told me "I didn't mean anything by it. That is the point, let the bottom create meaning in the experience."

Other ways to utilize this strategy can include the top wearing a mask that is silly, scary, gross, or of an authority figure. Alternatively, the bottom could wear a mask but in this case be aware of the nature of the mask. The possibilities with just masks are nearly endless, and what is more, you could combine that with wearing a costume or using other role-play props.

This story includes asymmetric information *mindfucking* because the bottoms didn't know what the masks were but the top and the audience did. This could easily be a degrading or ennobling *mindfuck* depending on the nature of the mask and how the person feels about wearing it.

***

Aftercare

Aftercare, for those that do not know, is what happens after any BDSM play. It usually involves stepping out of the roles you were playing in the scene, and caring for one another. Maybe this includes a blanket and a cookie, maybe it includes a conversation about how it went and that we are not role-playing anymore. With *mindfucking* there is a special component to aftercare that requires we "unfuck the mind."

Unfucking the mind is when we reveal the mystery, uncover the illusion, release the mind from mental bondage, and step out of our roles that were used for play. We must care for our partner, help them feel safe if they were made to feel unsafe in play, help them see hidden information, and step back into reality together.

We owe a tremendous debt to LARPers or people who participate in Live Action Role-Play for their development of techniques we can incorporate in aftercare for *mindfucking*. It may consist of as many as three distinct parts: epiloguing, de-rolling, and debriefing. In epiloguing also known as "game wrap" the top reveals secrets, explains content of the *mindfuck*, and perhaps finalizes the plot if there was one. With de-rolling, we discard character aspects and restore the players to who they are. Finally, with de-briefing we take time to capture any opportunity for learning and also make space for the discharge of emotion. Often done symbolically in LARPing by removal of costume pieces, make up, etc.

In BDSM play the process may not be so neat and tidy. Our partner might have just finished crying, or cumming, or cumming while crying. Due to this, the first step may be just to hold your bottom and tell them they are safe. This is Often partners can become non-verbal with such intense scenes and trying to communicate learning points while they are still in this state would be a pointless exercise. Other times or with other partners things might not be so heavy and you can go straight into discussions. Others still may need very little in the way of after care and your entire aftercare routine could consist of "You know I was messing with you right? Are you good?" For me personally, when the latter is the case, I need more than that for aftercare so I will arrange for cuddles with my other partners or friends after a scene. This is known as an "aftercare proxy."

Aftercare is essential in one form or another. Be sure to negotiate aftercare before a scene and be aware of any discrepancies in needs between you and your partner. The most important aspect when *mindfucking* is to take the time to be sure that ALL PARTIES INVOLVED know that the game is over.

***

Figure 6. LARPers in the Wild

Interlude #13 Mistress Cyan and the Skills Test

Mistress Cyan Saint James is the Headmistress at Sanctuary LAX Studios. I speak to her often as she has been my mentor for years. Once, we were having a conversation about my wife Queen Ana Algos and her moving up from Switch to Domme in a professional capacity. She revealed to me a creative *mindfuck* that she uses when evaluating ladies making such a transition.

One of the things that Mistress Cyan asks subs and switches that are interested in advancing to Dominant to do is hit her with a whip. It is common for a Headmistress to require a skills test of new Dominants but being asked to hit their boss is not so common. Now, from the outside this might not seem significant, but Mistress Cyan is their boss and also what many would describe as a big a fucking deal. Furthermore, she is never seen bottoming, only topping. Lastly, Mistress Cyan has a slender frame and very little body fat.

So, to ask these aspiring Pro-Dominants to hit her with a whip defies the expectations that she never bottoms and you can't hit your boss. It also serves to demonstrate to Mistress Cyan, how confident they are in their whipping skills.

So, this would be an expectation type *mindfuck* because no one was expecting that. It is also an ennobling type *mindfuck* because it is emboldening to know that you can "even hit the Headmistress with confidence."

***

Kinky Blackjack

Card games are excellent opportunities to exercise a *mindfuck*. Here is an example of adapting Blackjack for just these purposes. One-on-one kinky blackjack is an excellent strategy in the case of a couple that is composed entirely of submissives or switches. In this case anyone might be willing to top but no one wants to dominate. In this case the power is actually relegated to the cards. It is more of a *mindfuck* if the power is only perceived to be relegated to the cards. This can also be utilized for a standard Dominant and submissive pair or groups.

This strategy uses the perceived power *mindfuck*. The decision of what activity is done is left up to chance but not entirely. If your partner is less knowledgeable of blackjack and or statistics this can be used to your advantage. For those unaware of the game, I will paint a picture with the broadest strokes here:

- One person is designated as the dealer, who also plays the game
- Each player competes with the dealer only
- Each player is given two cards, one face up and one face down
- The objective is to get a value of 21
- Face cards are valued at 10 and an Ace is valued at 1 or 11 at the players discretion
- Any value greater than 21 is a "bust" or automatic loss
- The player can request additional cards "hit" or refuse additional cards by saying "stay"
- The player with the highest value hand not exceeding 21 wins
- The dealer has an advantage since they win if the other player busts before the dealer takes their turn last
(there are more rules but these shall serve for context if you are unfamiliar with the game)

So, in a one-on-one game of Blackjack the dealer begins with a slight advantage. Before the game begins each player (or just the D-type) should brainstorm BDSM or sexual play activities that they would enjoy doing/receiving. The 13 items are assigned to the cards, one to each card, like Ace for spanking, 2 for scratching and so on. I have compiled a full set of activities that I used for a play scene on page 105.

Now, the winner of any hand of Blackjack is left with two or more cards that suggest a certain activity. The winner can choose to do or have done to them any of the activities listed on the cards or pass. The *mindfuck* is one of perceived power. This is because the author of the activity list (what activity each card suggests) is in control of what is possibly happening, while it would appear that the cards are in power instead. Furthermore, since it would seem any activity is equally as likely to be selected as any other, there is another opportunity to confuse power. While each card is as likely as any other to be drawn (1/13 or 7.7%), it is not equally likely that any card would be in a winning hand. A, K, Q, J, and 10 are more likely to be in a winning hand than lesser valued cards, and so the activities assigned to those cards are more likely than they appear in a winning hand. In the example set of activities displayed, all genital sex activities are given face cards, this makes them more likely to be part of a winning hand and therefore more likely to be an activity selected.

The blackjack *mindfuck* can easily be done with multiple players. The rules are the same as before. Typically, in blackjack each player competes only with the dealer and not with the other players. This would lend itself to a co-bottoming situation in which one top is dealer and topping the rest of the players.

Another opportunity for multiplayer *mindfuck* blackjack is that the dealer is the Dom while the players are a mix of Tops and Bottoms. The dealer may for example win a hand against player number 3 that includes the cards 3, 7, and 10. If the dealer does not want to either tickle, paddle, or cuddle player three, they may say "player 3, paddle player 2." In this way the dealer is positioned as the Dom while others may top or bottom.

This setup does allow for bottoms to make some decisions. Many, especially the more submissive players may find this distasteful. On the other hand, if you find yourself in a room full of pansexual switches, which I am often lucky enough to do, this is an elegant solution for filling your evening with unexpected fun.

An Example of Activities for Each Card
2 - Spank
3 - Tickle
4 - Scratch
5 - Cane
6 - Taser
7 - Paddle
8 - Water Sports
9 - Whip
10 - Cuddle
J - Mutually Masturbate
Q - Give Head
K - Fuck
A - Anal

At the outset, the game may appear fair. As you can imagine, since it is a game that is played regularly in casinos, it is not. There is an advantage to the house known as the house edge. This can be leveraged for your benefit since there are innumerable rules designed to tweak the house edge for the benefit of the casino. The house edge is described in terms of a percentage. For blackjack the house edge may be as little as 0.5%, meaning that the game is very close to being fair. A list of possible rules and how they affect the house edge is easily obtained with an internet search.

Here is the benefit of using blackjack for this *mindfuck*. In the name of separating gamblers from their money, an incredible amount of research and development has been poured into understanding the probabilistic effect of different rules. So, if you are the dealer there are a myriad of ways to skew the odds in your favor.

There is also an opportunity to shift the odds in a less subtle way. One could for example get multiple decks and substitute some cards for another. This would make one activity more likely and another less likely. Alternatively, you could remove all of the 6's and add 4 additional Aces to eliminate the possibility of the taser card being drawn and double the chances of the anal card being drawn. No one said the game had to be fair.

Besides the actual logistics of the game, there are other opportunities to *mindfuck* in this scenario as well. You can utilize the perceived power type of *mindfuck* by wearing something official looking as many dealers do in casinos. You could be very knowledgeable (or appear to be) about the game. You could utilize the asymmetric information type of *mindfuck* by telling your players some of the rules but keeping others secret until it is useful to you. You could utilize the degrading or ennobling type of *mindfuck* by treating your players like a respected high roller or berating them for losing and making such insignificant bets.

***

Figure 7. Blackjack at the Casino

Sir Ezra's Box

Being that this book has been entirely composed during the 2020-2021 Covid-19 Pandemic, there have been substantial barriers to play. Many of my play partners are scattered across the country and travel has become a dangerous affair. Others are immunocompromised and the prospect of getting together exceeds a tolerable risk. My imagination, however, is not compromised and I continue to dream up new and interesting ways to *mindfuck* my partners, even if I do not know when I will get to act on these plans. For this reason, along with all of the *mindfucks* described in the book, I will include a hypothetical mindfuck. This will give you the benefit of seeing how a scene might be planned out that is more elaborate than some of the examples given previously.

The idea came to me when researching operant conditioning, more specifically the work of Dr. B. F. Skinner. His research with rats and pigeons was instrumental in developing what we know today of punishment and reinforcement and their effects on behavior. "Skinner's Box" was an experimental set up where a rat was introduced to an enclosure with an electrified floor, a food dispenser, a lever, signal lights, and a speaker. The box had several iterations and not every iteration had each of the described components.

    This and other experiments explored the effectiveness of positive and negative reinforcement and punishment (+P, -P, +R, -R). Positive punishment is when something is added to decrease a behavior. Examples include reprimand and spanking. Negative punishment requires something be removed to decrease a behavior. Examples of negative punishment are removal of privileges such as grounding or no TV. Positive reinforcement requires something be added to increase a behavior. An example of positive reinforcement is a tangible reward like a treat. Negative reinforcement requires something be removed as a way to increase a behavior. An example of negative reinforcement is when the smoke alarm is blaring until you remove the source of smoke. More information about this is easily accessible online by searching for B. F. Skinner or operant conditioning.

    What I propose is an adaptation of the Skinner's Box to what I call *Sir Ezra's Box*. My goal is different from Skinner's in that I am not bound by the pursuit of novel knowledge. In fact, I'm not required to learn anything at all in this endeavor. I am obligated to avoid actual experimentation, as my "subjects" will be human and there are several sets of ethical restrictions on how human experiments can be conducted. What I can do is role-play as an experimental psychologist as long as my participants are aware that it is not an actual experiment. My goal is not insight at all, it is the experience of the participant, myself and the possibly observers. The goal for myself and observers is pleasure and enjoyment as sexual sadists. The goal for the participant is any of the various emotions or sensations desirable as part of a *mindfuck* including: sexual pleasure, helplessness, frustration, pain, humiliation, degradation and any of other sensation a masochist might enjoy.

   In "Sir Ezra's Box" the subjects are human and so the box must first be substantially bigger than Skinner's Box. At first, I imagined a scaled-up version of Skinner's Box. Later I realized that I would want more flexibility to display the subject than a rigid box would allow. So instead, I imagine three walls covered by curtain with a wooden panel in one. This way myself and any observers have a good view of the bottom. The room in which the enclosure is placed should be entirely dark with exception to the interior of the box so that the observers or the larger environment do not serve as a distraction to the participant.

I imagine in the box will be a table, a chair, a dog training shock collar, a red indicator light, a green indicator light, a speaker, a dispenser, and a wand vibrator with a cord wired through the wall of the enclosure. The bottom is made to interact with the enclosure and not so much with the top directly. It is interesting to note that this scene set up is "covid-19 compliant" since the top and bottom are easily separated.

The bottom can be subject to punishments or reinforcements just like in Skinner's Box with the goal of performing a desired task or eliminating an undesirable behavior. The list of behaviors to reinforce or punish is nearly endless. I first imagined two tasks to "train" the bottom. The first is position training, where the bottom is made to perform either Gorean slave positions or perhaps yoga positions. The second thing that came to mind is dildo training where the bottom is conditioned to use the dildo in a way that pleases the top.

From Skinner's work we know that positive reinforcement is more effective in establishing a desired behavior than negative reinforcement. It is most effective in fact if the reward is unpredictable as in fishing or in slot machines. With Sir Ezra's box I am not obligated to go for actual behavioral modification but if I choose to make that my goal, I would use positive reinforcement. To do that I would either use the wand vibrator or a beep that can come from the shock collar. For the wand I would turn on the power whenever the bottom was doing the desired behavior such as demonstrating correct slave positions or using the dildo. I would use the tone for positive reinforcement if the bottom appreciated words of affirmation. I would let the bottom know ahead of time that the beep means good job, or I'm proud of you, or whatever accolade they respond well to. With the wand I would either power it on for a set amount of time, or use a roll of the dice to determine if it gets turned on, thus employing randomization to improve the effectiveness of the reinforcement. I would also have to make sure that the wand vibrator was a viable reward for the person. Some people don't enjoy the wand vibrator because it is very strong and they find extreme stimulation irritating.

For positive punishment I would use the shock collar to discourage unwanted behavior. As a side note, I don't encourage the use of a dog shock collar on a person's neck or chest, especially if the bottom has had any heart health issues or electronic implants. I would recommend instead attaching the shock collar to the thigh or ancle and also replacing the fur penetrating prongs with flat headed screws if possible. You want your bottom to be comfortable while you are torturing them after all.

    A good shock collar has a range of intensity and a conversation ahead of the actual scene about what levels are acceptable to the bottom is essential. That being said, an unpleasant shock can be a strong deterrent to a specific behavior. Perhaps if I'm doing slave position training and the bottom is apologizing every time their posture is corrected, a shock and a verbal reminder to not apologize might help. Or in the case of dildo training when they put the dildo down or take it out of an orifice, then a quick shock will let them know they need to change their behavior quickly.

    An example of negative punishment might be having the wand vibrator on consistently and turned off when the bottom either fails to hold the desired slave position or stops using the dildo.

    An example of negative reinforcement might be having the shock collar go off every 15 seconds unless they are in the correct slave position or in the case of dildo training, using the dildo.

Again, the goal here is not necessarily behavioral modification but everyone involved having a good time. Some of the above-mentioned activities would be wholly unpleasant to certain bottoms while others would enjoy it very much. The activities that would go on in Sir Ezra's Box would have to be negotiated specifically with each bottom. There is no magic combination of actions that could be conducted in Sir Ezra's Box that will be satisfying or effective for all participants.

As an alternative to the shock collar and vibrator, punishments and reinforcements could be administered simply by using indicator lights. We can communicate to our bottom that the red light means that you are not doing things correctly while the green light means that you are. Some bottoms are so eager to please that simply informing them they are off the mark is enough to motivate them to change behavior. Additionally, music can be used as a positive reinforcer, do the thing and get the music, fail and the music stops. For some, the silence can be deafening.

There is also the possibility of using a dispenser to dispense rewards. There are dispensers made for fish food dispensing that could be used to dole out small amounts of candy (nerds perhaps) to the bottom for a job well done.

The possibilities with this "experimental setup" are nearly endless. Others that come to mind are reducing someone's sense of modesty and pushing them to be more exhibitionistic, throat training, driving them to humiliate themselves in front of an audience, an interrogation, anal training, sisification...

The *mindfuck* here is many different things. There is a perceived power *mindfuck* when I wear a lab coat and role-play the prudent experimenter. There is potential for a humiliating or degrading *mindfuck* depending on what the bottom is made to do and how they feel about having an audience. The set-up of this being an experiment has a strong potential to be a perspective altering *mindfuck*. There could be a perspective alteration if for example I referred to the bottom as "subject 447" instead of by their name, or referred to them in the third person while addressing the audience. There is potential for an illusion type of *mindfuck* if I used the Shepherds Tone or Dark Shepherds Tone to manipulate the bottoms mood. It could be an expectation type of *mindfuck* if I housed this set up in some storage container at a yard by the pier and let them wonder what is about to happen in this remote, sketchy location.

All in all, this has the potential to be a versatile and dynamic setup for *mindfucking*. I am excited to build the first iteration. I've spoken to a few bottoms that are open to exploring this concept with me as soon as it is possible to meet up again. I hope that some elements of this setup appeal to you and that you might find a way to incorporate it in your play.

***

Interlude #14 The Philip K Dick-Move or Blade Running in the Dungeon

The premise is similar to the movie Blade Runner, in which robots, nearly indistinguishable from humans, are hunted down. Oddly enough, this was done in 2019, the year in which the original futuristic movie was set when it was released in 1982.

The experience was billed as a *mindfuck* class and taster to be held in person, at the Sanctuary LAX Studios dungeon on a Sunday afternoon. Forms were sent out ahead of time asking for people's fears, phobias, pet peeves and so on. Extensive warnings were issued to participants that the content of the class might be upsetting or disturbing and that if they were not willing to participate in the taster component that they were not welcome. Seats were limited to 40. Advertising explicitly stated that tickets were expected to sell out far in advance and no ticket would be sold the same day. Tickets sold out far before the day of the class.

    I greeted each guest upon entry to the event, each participant was asked to fill out an extensive consent form, and was assigned a paper bracelet with a two-digit number. The numbers were matched to the person's name on the RSVP list and they were allowed to enter the main hall. There was an area in the main hall by the stage where there were red velvet stanchions sectioning off an area. Participants were instructed to stand in the sectioned off area and wait for class to begin.

    After a short time, I took the stage to begin the class. "*Mindfucking* is a form of edge play" I said. "It is particularly dangerous because the risks and damage done can be unknown to both parties until it is too late. An excellent way to frame a *mindfuck* is within a game. A game is a useful context for a *mindfuck* because the game master can set intentions, objectives, rewards, punishment, values and so on. One thing we must be absolutely aware of, one thing you must always remember, something you must never forget is…" I stopped my lecture as an assistant came on to the stage to whisper something in my ear. Then in a surprised tone I addressed the audience again "Ladies and Gentlemen, I'm afraid our lecture has been canceled for the day. There has been a tragedy at Raytheon, just down the street. There has been an explosion, several people have died and several assets have escaped the facility. The assets are described as robots nearly indistinguishable from people. Due to this having happened 30 minutes before the beginning of our class, the assets may be among the audience members here today. We have several law enforcement personnel here to interview each of you individually to see if any of you are either involved in the incident or one of the escaped robots."

    Participants were then lined up and each given a card after volunteers demanded a response to the statement "tell me about your father." The card had three pieces of information on it. The first was their robot status. This either said:

        A) You know you are a robot
        B) You think you are a robot

C) You think you are not a robot
D) You know you are not a robot

The second piece of information was the Secret. The secret was either:
1) You are a murderer
2) You are a thief
3) You are a robot lover
4) You have no secret

Last was an objective based on the first two pieces of information. Examples of the objectives might be for D4 - Find the robot, for A1- Don't get caught, for B3 - Free the robots & cause confusion. Codes which indicated their identity were also written on their paper bracelet.

Participants were instructed to go back to the stanchioned off area and read an instruction sheet. The instruction sheet informed them that they were allowed to accuse any of their fellow participants of being a robot if they had two other participants to also agree to the accusation. Any accusation was tried by a Judge who was a dedicated volunteer. Those found guilty would be sentenced to jail. Being that we were in a BDSM dungeon we had a jail room readymade.

Participants were pulled one by one and interviewed by any of the 4 people who volunteered to be officers. Some were interviewed more than once but everyone was interviewed at least once.

After everyone had been interviewed, several people accused, some people jailed, and even myself being accused of being the robot, the game was called and everyone was invited to take a chair in the stanchioned area for a game wrap, epilogue, and de-roll. Secret identities were revealed, the plot was explained and several of the *mindfucks* were explained to the participants. All of the volunteers sat facing the audience panel style and we took questions on both the experience we just had and *mindfucks* in general.

The *mindfucks* here were extensive. I will name as many as I can and leave it to you to determine what type or types of *mindfucking* each example is.

- How people were dehumanized with the use of a number instead of a name
- How easily people will endanger others to protect themselves
- The interrogation by officers

- The fact that less than a quarter of participants had a motive congruent with the group activity
- The question about participant's fathers
- The interruption of the lecture
- The severity of the consent form (which had questions like "What is your worst fear?" and "Do you have any heart conditions?"
- People given permission to accuse each other
- The threat of being jailed

***

Conclusion

I hope that I have been able to illustrate the varied and diverse practices of *mindfucking* in BDSM. I hope I have shed some light on its origins and given some guidelines on how best to play as safely as possible. If this is your first time learning about *mindfucking* I hope it is the first step of a long journey of learning.

Mindfucking will continue to be a part of BDSM and the human experience. I hope this text has brought you one step closer to having the resources you need to have the most exciting and intimate play possible.

There were many other topics that touched on *mindfucking* but didn't quite make the cut, including mindfucking for spiritual practice, erotic hypnosis, a deeper dive into discordianism, tarot, other historic atrocities and experiments that come close to a mindfuck including the Salem Witch Trials, the Milgram Experiment, the Stanford Prison Experiment, Young Albert Experiment... I had considered discussing at length operant conditioning, social influence and other fields of study which seem to inadvertently delineate *mindfucking* in a way. As useful as it may have been to indulge in these peripheral topics, I figured it had more potential to distract from the central topic. Perhaps if there is sufficient interest, I will expand upon this book and touch on some of the above topics in the following edition.

My goal with this book was to help people have hot, sexy, and safer play. I hope this serves as a key, or more a key making kit, that you can use to unlock possibilities in your own mind and in your relationships. For me personally, this endeavor (and most everything I do) has the aim of establishing, and deepening connection. If you felt this book helped you connect with your desires, your fantasies, your partner or your community then feel free to reach out and let me know. Lastly, if you enjoyed this book feel free to leave a review of the book where you purchased or on my website at HouseOfAlgos.com.

Those interested working with me directly through my work as a Sex Coaching, BDSM Life Coaching, Dominant or submissive Training, joining a live group class or scheduling private classes can use houseofalgos@gmail.com or visit WhatsInMyKinky.com to learn more about these services and opportunities.

Additionally, those interested in being "test subjects" for Sir Ezra's Box, message the email above with subject line "Sir Ezra's Box." For those eager to try out a *mindfuck* feel free to visit houseofalgos.com/mindfuck-sample.

***

Bibliography

The Vintage Fetish and Fashion blog is the source of the vintage fetish photography in the book.
Karen, "Watersports" *Vintage Fetish & Fashion,* Flickr, https://vintagemusing.com/2019/08/12/watersports/, accessed January 2021.

This site gives a more comprehensive history of BDSM and Sadomasochistic practices throughout history.
Skyeler Huntsman "High Altitude History" *The Extended History of BDSM,* Montana State University, 26th April 2017, historymsu.wordpress.com/2017/04/26/the-extended-history-of-bdsm/. Accessed January 2021.

The source of quotes regarding the mindfucking in the South African education system.
Kai Horsthemke (2014) 'On Bullshit' and 'Mindfucking': an essay on mental manipulation in education, South African Journal of Philosophy, 33:1, 35-46, DOI: 10.1080/02580136.2014.892675

This book examines mindfucking from a philosophical perspective.
McGinn, Colin. *Mindfucking.* Acumen Publishing Limited, 2008.

This is the Planned Parenthood website. It is an excellent source of information and resources for women's reproductive health and the F.R.I.E.S. acronym for consent.
Planned Parenthood. "Sexual Consent." Planned Parenthood Foundation of America plannedparenthood.org/learn/relationships/sexual-consent. Accessed January 2021.

The KHN news website was the source of the Trump Mindfucking information.
Funke, D, & Sanders, K. "PolitiFact" *Lie of the Year: The Downplay and Denial of the Coronavirus*, Kaiser Family Foundation, 16 Dec. 2020, https://khn.org/news/article/lie-of-the-year-the-downplay-and-denial-of-the-coronavirus/. Accessed January 2021.

This site describes records of how thousands of Native American women, including some minors, were sterilized without their consent in only a few years.
National Library of Medicine. "Native Voices" *1976: Government admits unauthorized sterilization of Indian Women,* National Institute of Health, nlm.nih.gov/nativevoices/timeline/543.html. Accessed January 2021.

This page includes an interview with "silly revolutionist" Mathew silver. There is a written interview as well as several videos. The video that I used to pull the quote from the book is

the fifth one from the top. It can also be easily located because the cover of the video is the only one where he is wearing pants.
Antraeus de Herschia. "The Treasure Chest." *Mr. Wackadoodle and the Vortex of Love,* Blogspot, 26 Jan. 2015, http://treasurechestarrr.blogspot.com/2015/01/mr-wackadoodle-vortex-of-love.html. Accessed January 2021.

An article on the history of douching and how corporations prayed on the insecurity of women.
Stephanie Buck. "Timeline," *The Sexist, Toxic History of Douching,* Medium, 14 Aug. 2016, timeline.com/sexist-history-douching-bcc39f3d216c. Accessed January 2021.

This page shows an article describing how women are being forcefully sterilized in immigration detention centers in the United States CURRENTLY!
Brigitte Amiri. "News & Commentary" *Reproductive Abuse is Rampant in the Immigration Detention System,* ACLU, 23 Sep. 2020, ACLU.org/news/immigrants-rights/reproductive-abuse-is-rampant-in-the-immigration-detention-system/. Accessed January 2020.

This Wiki article describes the origin and history of a group which may or may not be

fictitious, the Discordians. I deny any allegations future or present that I am a member of this group.
"Discorordian Wiki" *Operation Mindfuck,* Fandom, Last edited 17 July 2020, discordia.fandom.com/wiki/Operation_Mindfuck#Ongoing_projects. Accessed January 2021.

This article describes the overdose information available for Niacin.
Katherine Zeratsky, R.D., L.D., "Mayo Clinic," *Niacin overdose: What are the symptoms?,* Mayo Foundation for Medical Education and Research, 22 April 2020, mayoclinic.org/diseases-conditions/high-blood-cholesterol/expert-answers/niacin-overdose/faq-20058075. Accessed January 2021.

Upton-Clark, E., "Teen Vogue," *Pranks as Political Activism: From the Yippies to TikTok,* Teen Vogue, 29 JULY 2020, teenvogue.com/story/pranks-political-activism-history. Accessed January 2021.

This article describes B.F. Skinner's work on operant conditioning and how +/- reinforcement and punishment work in comparison to each other.
Saul McLeod, "Simple Psychology," *What Is Operant Conditioning and How Does It Work?,* 2018, simplypsychology.org/operant-conditioning.html, Accessed January 2021.

This article examines how the LAPR community deals with the end of a game. Their efforts have unwittingly contributed to how we do aftercare and specifically how we unfuck the mind.
Maury Elizabeth Brown, Analog Game Studies, *POST-PLAY ACTIVITIES FOR LARP: METHODS AND CHALLENGES,* Wordpress, JUNE 3, 2018, analoggamestudies.org/2018/06/post-play-activities-for-larp-methods-and-challenges/. Accessed January 2021.

***

References and Recommended sources

National Sexual Assault Hotline
rainn.org/resources – 800-656-4673

National Domestic Violence Hotline
Thehotline.org - 800.799.SAFE

National Suicide Prevention Hotline
suicidepreventionlifeline.org - 800-273-8255

A list of books said to induce a mindfuck. It is important to note that these books induce a mindfuck as defined outside of BDSM.
https://everything2.com/title/Books+that+will+induce+a+mindfuck

This website is a directory of Kink Aware Professionals. This is a good place to find a kink friendly or kink aware therapist.
https://www.kapprofessionals.org/business-directory-2/

This side displays and describes Blackjack odds and the effect rules have on the house edge as described in this book.
https://www.gamblingsites.org/casino/blackjack/odds-and-probability/

Resources for BDSM friendly therapy
https://societyforpsychotherapy.org/an-introduction-to-bdsm-for-psychotherapists/

The National Coalition for Sexual Freedom is committed to creating a political, legal and social environment in the US that advances equal rights for consenting adults who engage in alternative sexual and relationship expressions.
NCSFreedom.org

This site is the Free Speech Coalition. In FSC's own words "Our mission is to protect the rights and freedoms of both the workers and businesses in the adult industry."
FreeSpeachCoalition.com

This site is Sanctuary LAX Studios, where Sir Ezra works as Director of Education. Sanctuary provides the largest dungeon space in Los Angeles for community events and private rentals.
SanctuaryLAX.com

    Queen Ana's Patreon is the best way to get access to her classes as well as additional educational and behind-the-scenes materials. Queen Ana teaches AT LEAST ten classes a month and becoming a patron on Patreon is a great way to stay on top of your kinky education. Visit Patreon.com/QueenAnaAlgos to join.
    She excels at making people feel accepted, important, sexy, and at helping others understand they have power, no matter what side of the slash they may be on in their kink journey. You can also visit QueenAnaAlgos.com to learn more about what she has to offer.

    Sir Ezra's website is HouseOfAlgos.com. This site is the best way to learn about Sir Ezra's services including coaching, mentoring, group and one-on-one classes, private sessions, party planning, and Dom or sub training. Additionally, Patreon Membership is the best way to get unrestricted access to the full set of recorded BDSM classes. Sir Ezra's Patreon is Patreon.com/HouseOfAlgos.

Made in the USA
Middletown, DE
04 October 2024

61429519R00080